The Human Factor: Why Employees Are Your Biggest Cybersecurity Risk

Jacob

Table of content

1. Introduction

1.1. Background

1.1.1 Cyber incidents today

The phenomenon of cyber incidents is frequent in many industries. (Golandsky, 2016). A cyber incident is an attack on an information system through hacking, computer viruses, email bombs, and other technological disturbances (Lee and Seo, 2019) that can result in a financial gain for the hacker (Swedish Civil Contingencies Agency, 2020). According to Swedish Civil Contingencies Agency (2020) annual report, Sweden is currently in a time of high technological development that is beneficial for society which makes it more effective, global, and technologically advanced through the constantly increasing digitalization. However, the development of cybersecurity has not followed the same rhythm as the increasing digitalization (Swedish Civil Contingencies Agency, 2020).

In a report made by Truesec (2020), based on data from medium to large organizations, the percentage of cyberattacks had increased by 67% during the first five months of 2020 in comparison with 2019, in Swedish organizations. Based on the Security & Defence companies Annual Report (2021), eight out of nine Swedish companies had suffered cyber incidents during the last year, and Sweden is the most exposed among the Nordics. Due growth in cyber-criminal businesses, the incidents have become more efficiently organized and strategic (Security & Defence companies Annual Report, 2021).

1.1.2 Cyber incidents in the future

The Swedish Ministry of Justice (2016) presents in their report that the increase of digital transformation results in higher risks, requiring a more significant effort to ensure security in the population. Therefore, they assert that technological development entails constantly evolving methods and tools to commit cyberattacks. Another report from the Swedish Civil Contingencies Agency (2015), states that some data goes through several legal and technical systems, which leads to the threats of a cyber incident being complicated to detect. Choo (2011) argues that lots of cyberattacks appear in distinctive and more destructive ways. He further mentions that an increased amount of such incidents is to be expected in the future, considering the criminal actors´ financial interest in some organizations, which incentivize them to acquire their confidential information.

1.2 Problematizat on

Cyberattacks are a threat to information security and the underlying reason behind it is the continuous increase in internet consumption by individuals and organizations (Zwilling et al., 2020). Today IT systems are no longer used to support the business, but it is instead a precondition for the businesses to function. What is happening among companies is that they today rely more on effective processes, people, and security technologies that are usually threatened by cyberattacks. To reduce the risk of the threats, companies are trying to support information security by using different technological solutions (Reeves et al., 2020). Despite that, the number of cyberattacks is still increasing in Europe (Reeves et al., 2020; Panou et al., 2017). The identified reason behind it is the increased management of humans that lack risk awareness and knowledge regarding the possible threats of cyberattacks (Reeves et al., 2020). Zwilling et al. (2020) and Lacey (2010) claim human error to be the weakest link in the cybersecurity chain. Further, Zwilling et al. (2020) describe that no matter what tool is being used to strengthen cybersecurity, the lack of awareness among the employees and especially leaders will outweigh the preventive measures that are being implemented (Zwilling et al., 2020).

Continuously, studies have highlighted the importance of leaders when it comes to raising risk awareness among employees, due to their ability to influence and control the company culture to be more risk aware (Braumann, 2020). To further minimize the risk of cyberattacks, there is a need for adequate knowledge and risk awareness about the threats in the companies. Risk awareness also includes the security behavior that is being adopted. Previous research has shown that there is a general lack of risk awareness and adequate knowledge regarding cybersecurity (Kovacevic et al., 2020). Hence, Zwilling et al. (2020) describe that large organizations develop higher awareness because they have more financial resources available and determined security policies that everyone follows.

Although companies develop cyber security measures and policies, they do not always work as planned, because people have rather not enough knowledge regarding the threats or they do not perceive the risks (Bada et al., 2019). Moreover, Lacey (2010) and Bada et al. (2019) describe that the company environment and culture have an impact on the perception and awareness of the risks. Bada et al. (2019) and Bontempo et al. (1997) continue by stating that it is unusual for Western countries to discuss risks. Instead, the emphasis by the management is normally on financial revenues and value creation, leading the companies to be generally less aware of the threats of cyberattacks, increasing their weaknesses (Bada et al., 2019; Hasan et al., 2021; Abraham et al., 2019).

Due to the lack of a proactive attitude from the top management, companies are exposed to cyber incidents. Thereby, there is a need for a company at a structural level to prevent cyber crises. Swedish Civil Contingencies Agency (2020) states that cybersecurity is mainly the responsibility of the top management and largely depends on their attitude towards it. They continue claiming that without an engaged leadership from the management, there is a risk for the cyberattacks to become complicated, resulting in a crisis. Besides, distributing the responsibility of cybersecurity to only security professionals and not comprehending the preparedness needed at an organizational level, is a deficiency that many companies have (Chatterjee, 2019).

In summary, the lack of risk awareness of cybersecurity at a managerial and structural level in companies has become a topic that requires strategic decisions. According to Goel et al. (2020), to avoid disincentivizing employees to participate in the organization's cybersecurity, a full commitment from the top management is essential.

This study will focus on highlighting the top management's role in maintaining functioning cybersecurity. As argued earlier based on previous studies, raising awareness about the topic is a crucial component for the company to have sustainable cybersecurity. Therefore, this book will be devoted to investigating the level of risk awareness in Swedish companies and analyzing the prioritization of *cyber risk awareness* by the top management as a crucial component for the pure existence of an organization. It will contribute with a realistic point of view based on data provided by experts, about risk awareness and the role the top management plays in it, to further corroborate previous findings, contributing to a higher understanding of the topic.

1.3 Purpose

The purpose of the study is to contribute to an increased understanding of strategic leadership's influence on cyber risk awareness.

1.4 Research questions

- What is the state of cyber risk awareness in Swedish companies and what are the influential factors behind risk awareness?

- Why should cyber risk awareness be treated as a top management issue?

1.5 Delimitations

The focal point of the scope of the study is only Swedish companies. Thereby, all empirical data is presented through the perspective of researchers, experts, consultants and CEOs anchored in one way or another, to the cybersecurity in Swedish companies and organizations. Further, this book does not differentiate between types of cyber incidents or crises. Instead, it proceeds from a general point of view investigating with a methodological approach the influential factors lacking awareness, but also the consequences it can give to give an understanding of their significance. Further, the actions the top management can pursue to enhance cyber risk awareness and improve cyber security are discussed. There is a logical connection between an increased knowledge and risk awareness and an enhanced level of cybersecurity, and these go hand in hand, throughout the book. Another delimitation is to investigate cyber risk awareness and its influence on private companies and exclude its analysis at a national level. Finally, when treating stakeholders, the starting point is mainly the clients. In this book there is often a logical connection between the terminologies cybersecurity and risk awareness or cyber risk awareness, referring to that a high cyber risk awareness results in a functioning cybersecurity, which is also why they sometimes are used together.

2. Theoretical framework

2.1 Cybersecurity and cyber incidents

"We believe that data is the phenomenon of our time. It is the world's new natural resource. It is the new basis of competitive advantage, and it is transforming every profession and industry. If all of this is true – even inevitable – then cybercrime, by definition, is the greatest threat to every profession, every industry, every company in the world." - (Rometty, 2015)

2.1.1 Cybersecurity

Cybersecurity and *information security* are in most times used as synonyms due to this overlap in certain aspects although there are minor differences between them (Von Solms and Van Niekerk, 2013; Eswaran and Vinayagamoorthi, 2019). Cybersecurity is a term that has a broader meaning, it implies the protection of things in the cyber environment that are vulnerable and have a significance to the company. Besides, it also considers the technologies that are used to store and secure the data (Eswaran and Vinayagamoorthi, 2019). Von Solms and Van Niekerk (2013) emphasize that cybersecurity is an overall concept that stands for the tools, policies, guidelines, risk management approaches, training, actions, technologies, and best practices that are implemented with a purpose to protect a company's assets. Information security on the other hand focuses on the protection of more specific information and its critical elements in a narrower sense. Not all data can be qualified as information (Eswaran and Vinayagamoorthi, 2019).

Information security can be seen as a part of cybersecurity that is narrowed down to the information and the protection of it (Eswaran and Vinayagamoorthi, 2019). Hence, the objectives of both cybersecurity and information security are to protect the availability of the data and information, which implies the protection of access to it. Further, the objective is to cover the integrity of the information and hinder the improper modification or destruction of the data. The last objective is to protect confidentiality, which includes the restriction to access the data by unauthorized parties (Von Solms and Van Niekerk, 2013; Radziwill and Benton, 2017; Eswaran and Vinayagamoorthi, 2019). Organizations that work systematically with information security have better use of their information and they avoid any additional cost that arises with insufficient security (Swedish Civil Contingencies Agency, 2020). This book uses the terminology *cybersecurity* in a broad context, covering the definitions within the category and so even information security.

2.1.2 Cyber incidents

A cyber incident is defined as an event in which an external party without permission enters the company's database to take part of its private information, because of insufficient cybersecurity. In this book, cyber incidents and cyber-attacks are used as synonyms. Previous research distinguishes between four types of cyber events. The first one is data breaches, which refers to the unauthorized revealing of the personal information that the company possesses. The second type is security incidents, that is, an attack directed at the company, the third type is a privacy violation, and this is about a violation of consumer privacy. The last type is skimming incidents which are about individual financial crimes (Romanosky, 2016).

Normally cyber incidents are predictable and there is room for preparation for them. Nevertheless, on occasions, cyber incidents could develop into a crisis, and in these cases, the level of damage caused is abrupt and immense (Golandsky, 2016). Although as long as a cyber incident is under control, the situation does not have to worsen. It is first when it gets to other domains and can no longer be handled by the already existing management tools when the problem occurs, and a cyber crisis is a fact (Prevezianou, 2020; Golandsky, 2016). Although there are different types of cyber incidents, this book covers them all from a general perspective, without any distinction. This is since the focal point of the study is from a management perspective, considering the top management's role in giving a company the knowledge, risk awareness and the organizational culture needed for a solid cybersecurity. Instead, the definition of cyber incident and cyber crisis is being provided to the reader to create background knowledge.

2.1.3 Complications of cyber incidents: Cyber crises

The cyber crisis is the kind that oversteps functional, political, and time boundaries; studies have therefore been conceptualizing cyber crises as transboundary (Boeke, 2018;

Backman, 2020). Cyber crises usually possess distinctive features that previous researchers have detected. The first feature that Prevezianou (2020) describes is that it takes time for the concerned party to detect the contravention and get an understanding of the threat. Due to a lack of clarity of the situation by the involved parties, a slow response is obtained. Hence, it implies that the threat is being underestimated by the leaders, which hinders them from taking the appropriate management tools, indicating their low level of awareness.

The second feature is time, in the sense of the speed of the expansion of the crisis, and the difficulty to determine both the start and the ending point of it (Prevezianou, 2020). It is also a characteristic that is crucial for the transboundary crisis according to Backman (2020). The author states that the escalation of the crisis is outrageously rapid and broad in the sense that it touches different domains. The third feature described by Prevezianou (2020) is human error, for instance, miscommunication that can cause huge penalties and worsen the situation. According to Singh & Kapoor (2016), the human factor is the weakest link in the security, which leads to serious vulnerabilities in the system that the attacker uses against the company. Nonetheless, as mentioned, escalates quickly to something unpredictable (Prevezianou, 2020). Therefore, the capability to manage cyber crises in a company is directly vital for its extinction or durability as an outcome (Golandsky, 2016; Kulikova et al., 2012).

Cyber crisis management, unlike general crisis management, demands the ability to handle higher quantities of information (Golandsky, 2016). Usually, a cyberattack occurs after several warning signs, which indicates that there is a build-up process to it. Most of the time a series of cyber incidents happen that in the end trigger the outburst of the crisis (Golandsky, 2016). According to Goel et al. (2020), not emphasizing the prioritization of cybersecurity has hindered important knowledge and worsened the management's decision-making. An organization thereby must set clear priorities regarding cybersecurity, and the senior management, that is the highest level of managers below the board of directors according to the Oxford Dictionary (2021), is to incorporate strategic and trustworthy decision-making that can support the company to protect its business functions. A lacking standardization and monitoring of the nature of attacks can lead to the organization taking significant cyber risks, resulting in bankruptcy. Managers need to be encouraged to discuss the topic and allocate adequate resources to minimize cyber risks at an organizational level (Goel et al., 2020)

2.2 Risk awareness

Our world is formed by two approaches, the real one and the cyber one, this is the perception that Peck et al. (2020) provide. Although they are independent, they are jointly connected. Businesses and private actors are in contact with the cyber world daily, through the internet. This leads to the threats and risks of vulnerable data leakage. Besides, consequences like damage to the company's reputation are to be counted on in these cases, (Peck et al., 2020). The authors, therefore, highlight the importance of the necessity for increased awareness and knowledge in the area. In line with increased risk awareness, incident management of cybersecurity requires an increased level of attention in organizations. The larger the organization is, the more complicated this process becomes, including a broader range of events, but also a higher number of them, which in turn challenges the management and its collaboration with other partners (Staddon and Easterday, 2019).

Continuously, some of the companies that suffer exposure to cyber risks to a higher extent are those whose activities are majorly dependent on information technology for their supply chain and product delivery (Gao et al., 2020). Moreover, cyberattacks have become more common due to companies and society's increased dependence on information technology. Worldwide, cyber incidents cost US$114 billion yearly, and taking into consideration the time loss for companies that work on recovering from the attacks, the number would closely be US$385. In other words, the quantity of companies that suffer from cyberattacks is increasing (Jang-Jaccard and Nepa, 2014).

2.2.1 Risk awareness & knowledge - Critical factors

It is important for the organizational members to be aware of digital activities, for instance, downloading software or any kind of information disclosure to third parties. This is because it can reveal confidential information about the company. However, security awareness is a perpetual learning process that takes place on an organizational level, where all individuals in the organization are included and some possess certain duties to manage it. This results in a need for the management to comprehend and design strategies to handle and improve the cybersecurity (Canepa et al., 2021; Alruwaili, 2019)

In many cases, the top management overlooks raising security awareness. Instead, a high number of organizations invest in new complicated security technology, and some of them even hire security professionals. Still, raising awareness about the risks of these technologies among employees and customers is not a prioritized task by the top management (Alruwaili, 2019). To raise awareness about cybersecurity, an understanding of how people generally perceive risk is crucial. At the same time, people, in this case, employees and even customers, need to be motivated to develop a will to create an understanding of the importance of this kind of security and to follow consultation from the management (Alruwaili, 2019; Bada et al., 2019). The role and responsibility of the top management are thereby decisive, based on a top-down approach, a framework that allows leaders to assign resources to affect strategic and optimized risk management. (Goel et al., 2020).

2.3 The top management's role

According to the Cambridge Dictionary, (2021), the top management is defined by the group of the most important executives in an organization. Employees base their perceptions of cybersecurity on the actions taken by the top management and if these are in line with their statements, (Ruighaver et al., 2007; Dang-Pham et al., 2015). When the top management communicates their risk perception to employees, the risk awareness in the organization increases (Braumann et al., 2020). Moreover, decisions regarding risk management are influenced and made by the top management and ensuring a proactive risk attitude among employees should be of high prioritization for them. This is since cyber security affects a company's objectives to be reached (Collier et. al., 2007; Braumann et al., 2020). Lee (2021) argues that cyber risk management is a question that requires holistic management in a company, meaning that managers are to take into consideration not only the technical aspects of it but also the human ones.

Golandsky (2016) claims that the prevention of cyber crisis is a process that is a part of crisis management of a company, which directs the responsibility of it to the managers. The management´s main responsibilities are to take the leadership by coordinating and contributing to the team building that is responsible for cybersecurity. The top management also is the ones who create networks and collaboration with companies including competitors. Further, the top managers also need to have skills to handle the operational problems, the employees, the development, and implementation of the strategies. However, the top management needs to delegate the responsibility to professionals who possess the adequate knowledge (Mikušová and Horváthová, 2019).

Furthermore, to prevent cyber incidents the management can implement suitable tools to achieve situational awareness among employees. This means that people know what is happening around them all the time so that they can find a way on how to react when the circumstances change (Golandsky, 2016). For that reason, companies also offer training intending to improve security awareness and to avoid human error (Aoyama et al., 2015). A cyber crisis scenario obligates a manager to comprehend the event but also to determine the strategies required to solve it (Golandsky, 2016). The managers need to understand the crisis since the tools are chosen to manage it depending on their perception of it (Prevezianou, 2020).

Nevertheless, managing a company's cyber risk awareness and cybersecurity is complicated, since there is more than one factor that influences it. These are primarily the top management, but also the IT support, the skills acquired in the organization as a whole, the collaboration with competitors, the organizational culture including awareness. Previous research has shown that there is a correlation between the top management´s support of data security and a reduction in the number of cyber incidents. This is caused by a higher commitment from the top management to implement sustainable information systems, which in turn results in successful information security, (Hasan et al., 2021; Daud et al., 2018; Kankanhalli et al., 2003). This commitment also leads to improved security governance and control, (Hasan et al., 2021). Furthermore, to enhance the employees' skills resulting in higher levels of data protection and minimizing its weaknesses.

2.3.2 Organizational culture

To maintain a sustainable level of risk awareness and thereby cybersecurity, continuous training, education, and risk awareness are required. In connection with that, the organization's culture regarding cybersecurity operations is essential (Kankanhalli et al., 2003; Kraemer et al., 2009). The top management is connected to all elements of the organization which according to Mitrovic et al. (2019), implies that changes in it affect every part of the company and not least the organizational culture. The authors further state that the top management has a more significant impact on the culture than the culture itself on the top management. Hence, the business's success depends on the tone from the top and the culture that they create in the first place (Mitrovic et al., 2019).

The reason why culture plays such an important role for a company is that it includes the norms, values, attitudes, and assumptions that have been developed by the members of an organization. It works as a filter that shapes new practices that are being implemented in the organization (Summerill et al., 2010). This culture helps them determine the meaning of their surroundings and the way they behave (Janićijević, 2013). According to Lacey (2010), the organizational culture has a great influence on the perception and the way of thinking of the organizational members. It further has a significant influence on knowledge creation, where it enhances the ability to create new knowledge through previous one. Further and based on institutional theory, data has indicated that the top management affects the employee's attitude towards the company's security strategies. Still, they must keep a moderate level of pressure to accelerate the knowledge and to raise awareness (Kwon, et., 2012).

2.3.3 Solutional actions by the top management

To attain enhanced cyber risk awareness and cybersecurity, the top management can collaborate with competitors in questions regarding cybersecurity investments, but also disclose information inwardly to raise awareness among organizational members, (Looi,

2005). In their article, Staddon and Easterday (2019), explain that collaboration with a diversity of stakeholders at different levels empowers companies to point out how incident management should be prioritized and reinforced. Nevertheless, the authors claim that cooperation with competitors and business partners creates a substantial vulnerability for big companies.

Another party that companies might collaborate with is suppliers and business associates, to share information to address certain patterns that indicate a cyber incident (Hasan et al., 2021). To disclose the potential cyber incidents, companies are to analyze previous attacks and dig deeper into the actual additional costs and results they have caused. This process facilitates it to understand the threats of insufficient cybersecurity and identify the requirements needed to build a solid one. Nevertheless, the threats of cyberattacks vary depending on the company sector and the solutions need to be adapted accordingly, (Gao et al., 2020).

2.3.4 Lacking cybersecurity - A background on consequences

On some occasions, cyber incidents can develop into a crisis, and in these cases, the level of damage caused is immense (Golandsky, 2016). A cyber crisis implies a situation in which an essential cyber asset is being damaged or exploited by an unwanted and external party (Prevezianou, 2020), which can end up affecting the company's value negatively. It can both ruin the organization's reputation and affect the stakeholders' confidence in the company (Vardarlier, 2016).

According to Security and Defense Companies (2020), 90 % of cyber incidents enhance a company's intangible costs and direct costs. These include technical investigation, legal fees and attorneys, devaluation of trade name, value of lost content revenue and many others. A high number of costs is also related to the stakeholders, for example, lost value of consumer relationships. Kamiya et al. (2020) states that when a cyber incident occurs the relationship between the company and their stakeholders' changes, due to the company's exposure to higher risks.

Today, maintaining valuable relationships depends on, inter alia, cybersecurity as a critical part of a company's Enterprise Risk Management (ERM), considering that cyber crises are a direct threat to the organization and its members. Damages include financial penalties, deteriorated reputations, and a decrease in stock value (Lee, 2021), but most importantly it destroys the whole business activity that relies on open digital communication. Hence, this makes cybersecurity no longer only a concern of the IT department, but it must be addressed strategically by the top management (Rothrock et al., 2018).

2.3.5 Lacking cybersecurity & relations with stakeholders

Kamiya et al. (2020), writes that companies collaborate with a wide range of stakeholders such as consumers, suppliers, or employees who trust the company with their personal information, including financial data about them. When a cyber crisis strikes, it results in the stakeholders requiring better terms during a transaction because they aim to compensate for the risk that they are taking by negotiating with an organization that unexpectedly can be a victim of a cyber-attack. Further, the consumers' reliability and trustworthiness of the company might be destroyed. For many organizations, the most important factor for their business survival and success depends on the trust that the consumers lay in the organization's security of their personal information. Therefore, companies need to protect the information the consumers give them access to. If the organization cannot assure that the data is being protected, previous studies have shown that 21 % of the consumers choose to abandon the company, or make purchases that are smaller than intended, (Raghavan et al., 2017).

In some cases, valuable relationships can even come to an end (Kamiya et al., 2020). Furthermore, it is stated that the consumer's perception of the organization is important because, generally when they think that the organization is having a crisis, then that is the case. To maintain a balanced reputation, the organization then needs to convince the stakeholders the opposite (Bakos et al., 2019). This in turn forces the organization to provide a response and explanation to minimize the legal issues, mitigate the financial harm, and possibly reduce the negative perception by the stakeholders (Chen and Jai, 2019).

Another consequence for a lacking cybersecurity is the lack of sufficient communication with stakeholders, causing negative emotions from them towards the company. These can further affect the brand reputation and the public trust negatively (Chen and Jai, 2019), ruining long-term stakeholder relations by a needle scale crisis (Bakos et al., 2019). The reason why reputational damage resulting in poor customer relations has such a great impact is that for companies, having a favorable reputation is equal to a valuable economic asset. It contributes to the company´s outcome by affording it with a competitive advantage (Sinanaj and Zafar, 2016; Fombrun and Riel, 1997).

Often, crisis events tend to draw attention from the media, resulting in a negative influence and judgments of the company. This in turn causes destruction of the company's reputation and thereby its competitive advantage, which can lead to enormous financial costs and in worst case bankruptcy (Sinanaj and Zafar, 2016; Colloeoni et al., 2011). According to Gao et al. (2020), there are other kinds of significant losses for an organization experiencing a major cyber crisis, however, this book local point is the stakeholders who influence the brand reputation and its importance for the company's survival.

2.4 Theoretical Model

2.4.1 Risk awareness

Based on the Cambridge Dictionary (2021), risk can be defined as a possibility of something bad occurring while awareness is being defined as knowledge where something exists of an understanding of a situation based on experience or information. Therefore, risk awareness will be defined in this paper in the following way: it is knowledge or understanding of something negative occurring that is based on previous experiences or information. The expression *cyber risk awareness* is also used in the book to refer to risk awareness in the field of cybersecurity.

One perspective of the process of risk awareness presented by Jen (2012), where different factors that are of importance when increasing risk awareness within an organization are shown. It consists of *inputs* which are factors that influence the organization to work towards increasing risk awareness, that according to Freeman and Cavusgil (1984) and Maharjan and Maharjan (2020) include the *stakeholders, uncertainty, and objectives.*

Thereafter, Jen (2012) and Sarathchandra et al. (2016) suggest some *tools and techniques*, through which the awareness can be enhanced. Lastly, Jen (2012) presents some *outputs* which are beneficial and can be obtained when the risk awareness and knowledge is raised.

Inputs

Stakeholders

The stakeholder theory divides the organizational stakeholders into two groups. The primary stakeholders are those who have direct interaction with the organization such as the consumers, shareholders, employees, suppliers, and regulators. The secondary stakeholders are on the other hand those who can affect the company but do not engage in direct transactions with it, these are academic institutes, social activists, neighbors, and advocacy groups (Freeman and Cavusgil, 1984). Nevertheless, the secondary stakeholders have the power to influence the adaptation of regulatory plans and policies whereas the primary stakeholders possess the power to influence the adaptation practices that make the organization compliant (Maharjan and Maharjan, 2020).

The authors continue by stating that the proximity of the stakeholders to the company also plays a role in the stakeholders' power to influence the company. This moreover implies that the organization needs to identify the important stakeholders and thereafter make a prioritization of them based on that. This prioritization facilitates it for the company to understand which stakeholders are assigned most of the influential power (Walker et. al, 2008). The stakeholders' influence not only affects the company's actions and decisions but is also connected to the achievement of its objectives (Freeman and Cavusgil, 1984).

Uncertainty

Uncertainty signifies unpredictable and unanticipated changes that occur in either the environment and/or the behavior (Hoffmann et al., 2013). Environmental uncertainty moreover implies the unpredictability of the environment including unexpected changes in for instance the exchange rate, natural disasters, technological unpredictability, etc. These changes force companies to adapt and in some cases adaptation problems occur. Behavioral uncertainty, on the other hand, is about sudden changes among the exchange partners that result in delayed deliveries, poor quality, or strategic manipulation (Hoffmann et al., 2013). No matter what type of uncertainty that the organization is facing, it is the key element of risk.

A high uncertainty results in higher risk, which previous studies have found is connected to decreased investment and consumption which overall leads to reduced economic activity (Istiak and Serletis, 2020). High uncertainty according to transaction cost theory implies higher costs and transaction risks (Hoffmann et al., 2013). Even with the uncertainty, the organizations are sometimes able to make predictions over future risks which can make them to some extent be prepared when a threat strike (Fielder et al., 2018).

Objectives

The objectives are another component that initiates the improvement of the risk awareness in the sense that the organization according to Naderpour et al. (2014) and Webb et al. (2014), sets objectives and sub-objectives to achieve a certain output. The objectives form the basis for the decision-making in complex and dynamic environments because it works as a guideline for further actions, Naderpour et al. (2014). They are shared by the whole organization which at the same time takes a role as a coordinator for the employees on all levels, including the lower ones. This also implies that every level of the organization possesses the right information to be able to take adequate actions towards the goal achievement (Webb et al., 2014).

Constraints

The constraints that Jen (2012) refers to is the resource availability which always entails risks. Acar et al. (2019) defines constraints as an external factor that is being imposed in the form of a regulation, deadline, requirement, and resource scarcity. However, studies have shown that limited access to resources can foster creativity where people are being challenged and motivated to overcome a particular obstacle (Sonenshein, 2014; Pindek et al., 2019). From another perspective, constraints can also be pursued as hindrances where a lack of resources or equipment can cause stress and lack of performance among the employees (Pindek et al., 2019).

Tools and Techniques

Tools and techniques refer to methods to apply as a solution to increase risk awareness and therefore knowledge. One perspective that is presented by Mondino et al. (2020) is to raise the level of experience among the employees by either hiring already experienced individuals or by implementing simulations, case studies, or mentorships. Hence, the authors state that a higher level of experience contributes to an increase in knowledge resulting in a higher perception of the threats. Jen (2012) states that another method is to increase technical skills by training, feedback, supervision, or mentorship. Swedish Civil Contingencies Agency (2021) on the other hand states that some technical security measures increase protection against cyberattacks, but they also claim that systematic security analysis is irreplaceable, and that technical measures should be done as only a minimum. This is further compatible with the next perspective claimed by Sarathchandra et al. (2016) and Jen (2012) namely to increase the knowledge of risk management by training, having meetings that focus on risk identification. Sarathchandra et al. (2016) further states that sufficient knowledge creates a secure culture. A point of view that can be implemented according to Sung & Hanna (1996) is to normalize risk tolerance by defining the organization's risk level, providing the organizational members' simulations and examples. The authors further state that risk awareness increases with proper education. The fifth and last method that the risk awareness model presents is to enhance communication skills by training and coaching (Jen, 2012).

Outputs

Outputs refer to the benefits obtained with an increase in risk awareness. The model presents six benefits. The first one is increased accountability which is a greater understanding among the stakeholders regarding their role, responsibilities, and participation in risk identification (Harclerode et al., 2016). Another benefit that is presented by Jen (2012) is an increased identification of risks due to greater knowledge and awareness around it. This also implies that the risks are recognized quicker before they become an issue. Furthermore, the third benefit that an increase in risk awareness brings is gained experience among the stakeholder, which further leads to better risk assessment (Forno, 2019).

The fourth benefit that the model presents is better decisions, meaning that higher-risk awareness gives a better assessment and accuracy for the management when deciding (Jen, 2012). The fifth benefit that is being presented is following the appropriate approach, meaning that the top managers can shape the solution that is being made during the risk response. Lastly and the final benefit is increased performance, due to better knowledge, which leads to ameliorated quality in risk management. As a consequence, improved efficiency and performance among employees are achieved (Jen, 2012).

Figure 1: Risk Awareness Model (Recreated from Jen, (2012))

2.4.2 Tone from the top

The tone from the top has originated from the accounting practices with a purpose to ensure ethical and professional behavior among the company's members. Although later, it has evolved into a broader concept and therefore spilled over to the management practices (Schwartz et al., 2005). The tone from the top presented by Braumann et al. (2020) is viewed as an informal control practice that includes the values, beliefs, and traditions that can directly influence the behavior of a specific group of people. It is at the same time a powerful tool of culture control that in an organizational context can influence the behavior of the employees in different situations (Braumann et al., 2020; Merchant and Van der Stede, 2017).

The tone from the top has shown to be an impactful driver for a risk-aware culture (Braumann et al., 2020; Collier et al., 2006), it can be seen as a control practice that focuses the organizational attention on the risks to increase and strengthen risk awareness (Braumann et al., 2020). The tone from the top begins with the CEO and his/her position regarding issues like ethics, risk awareness, knowledge, and organizational culture, which is then further mediated downwards to the rest of the company (Kelly, 1990). Having this stated, the tone from the top focuses on the CEO's attention towards risk management from several approaches amongst the top-down approach, which is the one focused on in this book. It means that the commitment and behavioral expectations related to the risk issues are communicated from the top management, down to the employees.

Based on Beasly et al. (2005) the senior management's role is critical for the organization´s Enterprise Risk Management (ERM) when it comes to deploying it in the whole company. Enterprise Risk Management refers to a business strategy implemented to identify and prepare for any danger against the company. Additionally, Beasly et al. (2005) claim that defining clear roles and responsibilities, has been shown to impact a company´s ERM positively. Furthermore, a high-risk awareness and an extended knowledge about risk as a topic among the top management, has resulted in an increased level of deployment of risk management in the entity. Evidence has also shown that the involvement of the CEO and the CFO, is associated with an extended deployment of ERM throughout the company. Thereby, the tone from the top coming from the board of the senior leadership is decisive to both the implementation of ERM and the practices of it (Beasly et al., 2005).

Kelly (1990) also presents that tone from the top is crucial when setting the company's moral tone, namely the organizational culture, and the CEO is seen as a standard-setter and an example to follow, by the whole company (Kelly, 1990). As a consequence, the company's culture reflects the actions of the CEO and the top management, which can either be positive or negative for the organization itself. The objective is the creation of a transparent and trustworthy atmosphere in the company which increases open communication between levels, resulting in higher awareness (Biegelman and Biegelman, 2011).

According to Braumann et al. (2020) and Biegelman and Biegelman (2011), it is the tone from the top that sets the basis for risk management and the appropriate level of risk awareness in the organization. When dedicating their attention to risk issues, supporting risk management processes, and encouraging communication they can influence the organization. This is because if the leaders of a company put their effort, resources, and time on risk issues, leading by example, the rest of the company will follow (Braumann et al., 2020). Moreover, it is the internal culture that creates the framework of how risk is perceived at an organizational level but also sets the bar for the appetite for risk-taking. As responsible for the risk management strategy, the top management chooses how the risks are mitigated. An example can be to control activities based on policies that assure effective risk responses Collier et al. (2007).

Although the tone from the top does not work in isolation, but rather in a system interacting with others (Braumann et al., 2020; Beasley et al., 2005), the responsibility lies on them to communicate the importance of risk management (Zeier Roeschmann, 2014). This does not exclude that there is a complementary relationship between the tone from the top and the interactive control (Braumann et al., 2020; Mundy, 2010). Interactive control refers to the two-way dialogue, which can occur in the form of a discussion of the performance measures and budget data in meetings between the top management and the employees (Braumann et al., 2018).

The reason for both the top management and the employees to get involved in discussions regarding performance according to Braumann et al. (2020) and Mikes, (2009) is to actively participate in the decision-making and to regularly remind the employees about the risk issues. Roberts, (1990) states that sometimes the risk questions tend to be suppressed by the middle managers where the threats are presented at the convenience of the middle managers, which limits the knowledge shared and the participation in discussions. In turn. it hinders the development of risk awareness (Roberts, 1990). Therefore, the tone from the top needs to ensure that the risks issues are relevant to discuss among the employees so that the risk awareness is constantly developing. Besides, it leads to constant learning for the top management themselves because the focus is put on the information that both the budget and performance measures contain (Braumann et al., 2020).

2.5 Theoretical conceptualization

The objective of cybersecurity and information security is to cover the integrity and forbid improper modification of the data. On occasions when a cyber incident occurs, an external party enters a company's database without permission causing leakage of the company's private information. Sometimes a cyber crisis is developed causing a high level of damage, by spreading to other domains and thereby being uncontrollable by the management. Further, the weakest point when it comes to managing a company's cybersecurity is the human factor. Therefore, the company's top management need to prioritize knowledge and strategic trustworthy decision-making to protect their core, that is the business. If the top management oversees allocating resources to minimize cyber threats, the organization might be taking significant risks that are directly linked to a potential bankruptcy.

Continuing with the top management´s role, the power lies in their hands to implement the tools to achieve an enhanced awareness among employees within the topic. However, managing a company's risk awareness and cybersecurity is not a simple task and it is influenced mainly by the top management's actions related to knowledge, collaboration with competitors, the organizational culture etc. Evidence has shown that the top management has a high impact on the organizational culture that in turn influences the employee's attitude towards the company´s security.

In cases where the top management fails to maintain a sustainable level of cybersecurity, significant consequences are potentially caused. The relations with stakeholders can be destroyed. The stakeholders trust the company with their personal information and if such information is revealed to unauthorized parties, the company's reputation is ruined. As a following consequence, stakeholders might end transactions with the company and the consumer's perception of it changes negatively. It is also important to have continuous communication with stakeholders to avoid negative emotions from their side causing reputational damage. For a company, having a favorable brand reputation is equal to a valuable economic asset.

To avoid possessing a lacking cybersecurity, the top management are to make decisions such as collaborating with competitors, stakeholders, business associates and suppliers. Additionally, the company can disclose information inwardly to raise risk awareness among the organizational members. Another approach is to thoroughly analyze the cyber previous attacks and identify the costs they have caused to facilitate understanding the actual threats and manage them. Today, cyberattacks have become a crucial part of companies due to society's increased dependence on information technology, resulting in an increased number of attacks directed towards companies. Therefore, risk awareness is a critical component to consider, including an overall learning process about the risks and threats existing, at an organizational level. This leads once again to highlighting the role of the top management to not overlook raising security awareness and only invest in security technologies instead as the situation is today. Here, a top-down approach by the senior management is to be applied, where there is a need to understand how the employees perceive risks and how to motivate them to comprehend the importance of a functioning security.

2.5.1 Creation of conceptual framework

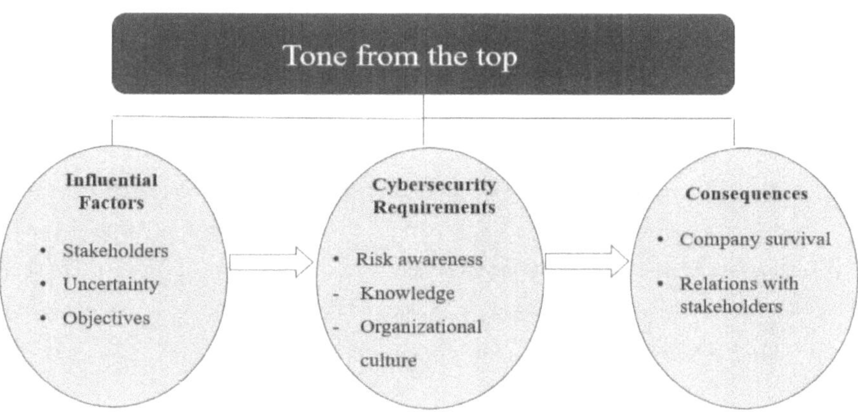

Figure 2. Visualization of the theoretical conceptualization

The theoretical conceptualization that has been developed in this study is primarily based on the *Risk Awareness perspectives* presented above and *the Tone from the top* earlier explained in *Chapter 2*. The *Tone from the top* shows that the top management is crucial for the whole risk awareness process, characterized by an influential role regarding the company's risk awareness and the consequences following (Braumann et al., 2020). The

Tone from the top as a theoretical model is thereby given a major character in the study, considering that it mainly comes from the senior management, also referred to as the top management in this book. Its members possess a managerial role in a company, resulting in them having the power to influence every component of it. Hence, in this study, the *Risk Awareness* perspectives presented are seen as one among other components that the *Tone from the top* has the power of. It is thereby the *Tone from the top*, that controls the risk awareness of the company. This perspective is reflected in the conceptualization by placing the *Tone from the top* above all elements of the *Risk Awareness* perspectives since its function is to control and manage the whole process of risk awareness in a company.

Consequently, both the theories presented in *2.4, Theoretical Model*, the *Risk Awareness perspectives* and the *Tone from the top* have undergone modifications, to develop a conceptualization suitable for this study. Starting with the *Tone from the top*, our emphasis in the conceptualization is that it is a strong tool controlling both the company culture and the behavior of employees. It can also increase the company's knowledge and risk awareness. An important aspect taken into consideration is that the *Tone from the top* starts with the CEO, and our study focuses on top-down risk management. Here, the involvement of the CEO and many times also the CFO has been shown to impact the company´s ERM positively. Since the Tone from the top, consisting of the senior management, has a decisive role in implementing ERM, it also sets the basis of it. Worth mentioning is that sometimes, risk-related problems might be suppressed from the middle management, which highlights the importance of the involvement of the top management in risk issues. The tone from the top is the controlling organ of the risk awareness existing in an organization.

Moving forward to the *Risk Awareness* perspectives in the conceptualization, some exceptions of the components of each box have been made, due to its lack of relevance to this study. The *Risk Awareness* perspectives are further seen as a process, starting from certain inputs, put into operation, and used as certain tools and techniques, which in turn gives outputs. The process is reflected by the arrows between each box. To simplify identifying and categorizing in the empirical data concerning the theoretical framework, the title of each box has been modified; Input → Influential factors, Tools and Techniques → Cyber Security Requirements and Output → Consequences. Nevertheless, the theoretical function of each box is kept the same.

When it comes to the first box, the focus has been put on primary stakeholders who as mentioned have an impact on the company's achievement of objectives. Further, uncertainty and especially the technological one is considered as a key element to minimize risks. This is since a high uncertainty is connected to an increased risk, which can result in decreased economic activity, based on the perspectives of *Risk Awareness*. Uncertainty can hence be reduced by preparation for future threats. Another factor included is the objectives since they form the basis for the decision-making and facilitates it to take adequate actions. When it comes to Cyber Security Requirements, containing methods to enhance cybersecurity, the third, fourth, and fifth methods in the *Risk Awareness* perspectives have been used as a starting point to our conceptualization. These methods include for instance raising risk awareness, normalizing risk tolerance, and increasing communication, which in this case have been summarized in the following concepts: *Risk Awareness, Knowledge, and Organizational Culture.*

As for the consequences including the benefits obtained because of functional risk awareness, the concentration has been put around the fourth, the fifth, and the sixth point. Practically, taking better decisions, knowing the context of risks, and having better knowledge about it, give improved relations with stakeholders and, thereby company survival as a result.

3. Methodology

3.1 Research Strategy

The scientific research method used to carry on this study is qualitative, intending to interpret non-numeric data that respond to the questions "how" and "why", instead of analyzing numeric information (Alvehus, 2013). In the case of the study, this methodology facilitates it to investigate and understand the *state* of cybersecurity in Swedish companies, the main factors that influence it, and to address the *crucial role* of top management for maintaining sustainable cybersecurity. The qualitative research method´s purpose is to display the complexity of the situation, providing a depth-understanding of the topic (Babbie, 2014). The methods were therefore found suitable to reflect the complexity of our research questions, to describe the state of risk awareness of cybersecurity, its influential factors and the consequences of a lacking cybersecurity among Swedish companies and to address the significance of top management´s role in it. The research questions of this study possess a descriptive character and intend to illustrate data based on words that require interpretation, which are some of the characteristics Bryman and Bell (2011) describe as a qualitative method.

3.2 Research Approach

There are two main research approaches in scientific research, ontology, and epistemology. Epistemology puts greater importance on what is knowledge and who can be the knower while ontology focuses on researching what is reality or nature (Bryman and Bell, 2011). Each research perspective has a research position that was found suitable for this study. In the ontological research perspective, there is the position of constructivism that implies that different phenomena are dependent on social factors. Social phenomena are a product of social interaction that influences behaviors, and due to that reason, it needs to constantly be revised. Within the epistemological research perspective, there is a research position of interpretivism, which means that the researcher interprets the data, and it means that he/she will always be a part of the study because the data will never be fully objective (Bryman and Bell, 2011).

We believe that both constructivism and interpretivism are the starting point of this study, which is further based on the nature of the research questions. Regarding constructivism, we are investigating the role of the top management in maintaining awareness about cybersecurity, in which the awareness is treated as a social phenomenon. Awareness refers to the knowledge that something exists (Cambridge Dictionary, 2021) which is created through learning in an educational setting but also by experiencing a particular situation. (Marton and Booth, 2013). We are further trying to describe the state of risk awareness, the influential factors behind it and the consequences of a lacking cybersecurity based on the perspectives of our respondents, which is further related to constructivism. However, even though we as authors are aiming to treat the data as objectively possible, our interpretations of the answers and the theory providing this study is impossibly excluded, thereby the interpretivism has also been used as a scientific approach. Due to our research design, explained in *3.3.1. Semi-structured interviews*, our interview questions were adapted to the respondents' answers and our interpretations of them.

3.2.1 Abductive approach

Alvehus (2013) makes a distinction between three research approaches, inductive, deductive, and abductive. The inductive approach according to Elo and Kyngäs (2008) and Alvehus (2013) begins with an observation that aims to contribute to the development of the theory at the end of the research. The deductive approach on the other hand starts with the development of a hypothesis that is based on already established theory. The aim of this approach is to test the hypothesis on the empirical data. This means that the inductive approach is contrary to the deductive, both starting at the opposite end of the research. The research processes that have been carried out in this book do neither fully agree with any of these two approaches. This book rather falls between both because it is neither based on a hypothesis nor is the aim to contribute with a new theory. Therefore, the approach that was found most accurate for this research is the abductive approach. This approach according to Alvehus (2013) implies a constant shifting between the empirical observations and theoretical considerations that at the end leads to a successive development of an understanding of the research.

Our research starts with going through the current literature on cybersecurity to get an understanding of the subject. This step contributes with the base knowledge that was needed in the development of the interviews to collect the empirical data. The literature review gave us a knowledge base to establish the design of the interviews in which we decided to focus our questions on cyber risk awareness, security and the top management's role and their responsibilities. After that we moved forward with the conduction of the interviews. From the empirical data that have been obtained during the first interviews we have acknowledged that there is a crucial relation between risk awareness and the responsibilities of the top management that we have to take into consideration. Together with additional literature research it led us to the development of the theoretical framework and the theoretical conceptualization that is presented in *Chapter 2*, that shows the relation between the tone from the top and risk awareness.

Continuously, when the theoretical framework was developed, and the empirical data collected, the analysis started in which the empirical data was analyzed based on the theoretical conceptualization, finding differences and similarities, and contributing with findings. This back- and- forth process between the empirical data and the theory let us land in conclusions about the relation between the top management and risk awareness and on the current state of the risk awareness in Swedish companies. The abductive approach helps understanding the empirics in the light of the theory (Alvehus, 2013). During the research process we could therefore keep a balance between the empirics and the theory, which led us constantly adjusting them to each other to meet the purpose of this study.

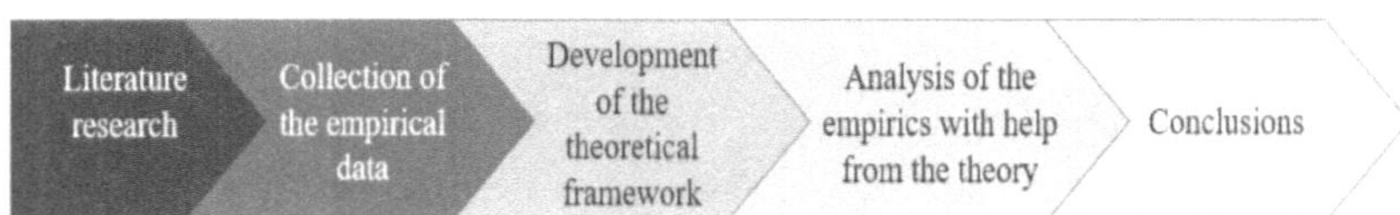

Figure 3. Visualization of our abductive approach

3.3 Research design

3.3.1. Semi-structured interviews

The semi-structured interviews imply that the researcher has a previously prepared interview guide that consists of either questions or topics that are intended to be asked in the interview. Despite that, the researcher has the freedom to ask the questions in the order that is most suitable for the specific interview which means that there is no obligation from the researchers' side to follow the schedule to the letter (Bryman and Bell, 2011). This method has been chosen, to adjust the interview according to the respondent and to obtain descriptive data that is explained deeply by the respondent when asked to give a nuanced perspective of a certain answer. Moreover, all respondents that participated in this study possessed a high level of knowledge about cybersecurity, due to their professional background in it. This allowed them to deliver a broad picture of the state of cybersecurity and the top management's role in it in Swedish companies. The semi-structured interviews even allow the respondents to influence the interviews (Alvehus, 2013), which in our case gives a positive impact due to their broadness of knowledge. Further, they allow the interviewer to listen carefully and participate actively in the discussion (Alvehus, 2013), something that raises the quality of the interview.

3.4 Data collection

3.4.1 Selection of respondents

The selection process is based on a strategic selection which according to Alvehus (2013) implies a selection process that is aimed to select participants with certain experiences that can provide the researcher with specific information. In our case, we are studying cybersecurity, risk awareness and the top management which means that the selected respondents must possess experiences and knowledge that can be related to the study. Therefore, when selecting the respondents, the main criteria that was taken into consideration was that the respondent is either currently working with cybersecurity or has several years of experience in the field. It was of importance to get in touch with people that have a lot of knowledge and experiences so that we can get information that is well-founded and trustworthy. We also put great emphasis on both, including experts from the private sector that work as consultants as well as researchers from different governmental research institutes and international science parks. The reason for that is that they, by having different work experiences, can provide us with different perspectives on the subject.

To get in contact with this specific kind of respondents we were provided with a list of companies and authorities that work with cybersecurity daily. The list was compiled by a Science Park in Sweden. After a selection of the persons and companies that were found interesting, we began to reach out to them by either phone calls, LinkedIn, or E-mails. After three weeks we got in contact with eleven people that agreed on an interview that took place during the following two weeks.

Collecting the empirical data, the prioritization was focused on finding the relevant interview respondents, who were able to give detailed and developed answers to the interview questions formed to fulfill the aim of the study. Therefore, the respondents needed to possess significant knowledge about the topic of cybersecurity, by having work experience directly related to cybersecurity tasks, or managing employees in the security department of their organization. Alvehus (2013) describes that a heterogeneous selection contributes to a broader insight into the studied phenomenon and an increased nuance of the data. In respect to that, the selected respondents come from different kinds of backgrounds including consultancy companies, science arenas, or even employees responsible for cybersecurity in the area of national protection. This provide us with different perspectives on the subject. It is important to highlight that the choice of respondents did not follow the traditional way of deciding which companies to include in the empirical data. Instead, the focus was on choosing respondents with the right knowledge and taking the company or the organization into consideration as a second priority. However, all organizations that the respondents belong to, have relevance and a connection with operating in cybersecurity. To protect the respondents' integrity, a decision was made to keep them anonymous. The following table presents the respondents, assigned a letter from A to K, their current job title, and a brief description of their job.

Table 1: Shows an overview over the respondents, their job title, description, and employment.

Respondent	Job Title	Job Description	Employment
A	Cyber Security Senior Consultant	Works on raising awareness about cybersecurity among Swedish companies.	Private company specialized in cybersecurity, risk management, and crisis management
B	Cyber Project Manager	The project focused on raising cybersecurity awareness among companies.	Research Arena directed to spread knowledge to companies in topics like cybersecurity.
C	Cyber Security Manager	Works with developing and maintaining the cybersecurity of the company.	Private company.
D	Cyber Security Researcher	Works on financing cyber projects for companies to raise awareness on the topic. Former cyber officer.	Research Arena whose aim is to raise risk awareness regarding cybersecurity among Swedish companies
E	Coordinator of an innovation institute in cybersecurity	Leader of cybersecurity innovation in the institute.	An institute that through international collaborations ensures the competitiveness of Swedish Businesses.
F	Cyber Security Senior Consultant & Chairman of the Armed Force's cybersecurity	Consults companies in questions regarding cybersecurity	Swedish IT company that provides digital services and system developments for other companies and organizations.
G	CEO former Cyber Manager	Provides other companies with the right tools to handle their cybersecurity	A consultancy company that develops IT security.
H	CEO	Provides clients with system developments to manage their cybersecurity.	A company specialized in cybersecurity management
I	Information Security Consultant	Solves clients' problems regarding cybersecurity and is responsible for external monitoring	Develops the IT infrastructure.
J	Information Security Consultant	Builds up information security programs and gives advisory to clients	Reduces cyber exposure with cybersecurity assessments.
K	Cybersecurity professional	Develops adequate cybersecurity	Handles the cybersecurity of the country.

3.4.2 The interviews

Bryman and Bell (2011) assert that the quality of the interviews can be enhanced when physically making it possible to read body language etc. However, due to the COVID-19 pandemic, this was not possible. To still be able to have a natural interaction with the respondents, all interviews except one took place through an online video tool. The one mentioned was made through a phone call. Before every interview, the respondent received a description of the study and an overview of the questions in a document to be able to prepare their answers, as preparation from both interview parties is required for a successful interview according to Bryman and Bell (2011).

With the receiving of the respondent´s consent, the interview would be recorded as an audio file. The function of recording the interviews was to facilitate the management of the information and to minimize the risk of excluding information due to human error from the interviewer's side. In the report, all respondents have been managed anonymously, including their company or organization, which according to Bryman and Bell (2011) is important. The duration of the interviews was approximately 45 minutes each, with an exception for two of the respondents who wished and could contribute with more information based on their expertise and interest. One of these interviews proceeded for an hour and another one lasted approximately 50 minutes. A total of 11 different respondents participated in the interviews. One of the respondents had particularly interesting information for our study, possessing a varied background and work experience in the subject of cybersecurity risk management. Due to that reason, the respondents were interviewed twice, providing us an in-depth understanding based on the interview questions.

3.4.3 Interview structure

Designing the interview guide, the questions were divided into three sections with the following designations: cybersecurity, risk awareness, and responsibilities. To start the first part, a short presentation of our research was made and questions about the respondents' background and connection to the topic of cybersecurity were asked, as Denscombe (2014) recommends. Opening questions of this character tend to create an openness between the interviewer and the respondent Denscombe (2014). The interview questions were formed to be open-ended and easy to understand, which is what Britten (1999) asserts as appropriate interview questions.

Furthermore, the focal point of the first section aimed to understand why it is important for a company to have a stable cybersecurity and whether they considered the state of risk awareness and knowledge was sufficient in Swedish companies. The second part of the interview focused on the management's responsibilities regarding organizational culture, knowledge and risk awareness and their significance for the cybersecurity of the company. The interview questions of this section aimed to create an understanding of the responsibility the top management possesses and takes in raising risk awareness and taking serious actions to reduce the risks of cyber incidents. The last part of the interview discussed the influential factors of risk awareness, the requirements needed to maintain a sufficient level of cybersecurity and the consequences of a lacking cybersecurity.

3.4.4 Transcription

We made the decision to record the interviews and to transcribe them continuously between the interviews. The weakness that the recording of the interview can bring according to Alvehus (2013) is that it can limit the participants' way to respond, where they may not feel comfortable enough to share a certain type of information. Therefore, it was crucial for us to get the respondents permission to record before the interview. We also made sure to inform the participants about the intentions to record the interview, in the interview guide that they received before the interview took place. Beyond that, this method was very beneficial for us because we had the possibility to go back and listen to the recordings at any time during the research process. It also facilitated the registration of the data after the interviews. Hence, during the interviews it became easier to mainly focus on the respondent and what was being said. The interviews were held in Swedish and were therefore transcribed in Swedish as well to further translate the relevant content to include in the empirical findings. It took approximately 50 hours to transcribe 12 interviews that lasted approximately 50 minutes each. This estimation is based on Bryman and Bell (2011) claim that one hour of speech takes around five to six hours to transcribe.

3.5 Analytical method

The analysis of the empirical findings is presented in *Chapter 5* of the book, in which the empirical data is analyzed with help of the theoretical conceptualization that has been developed in *Chapter 2*. According to Alvehus (2013) the analysis process consists of three working steps, these are data sorting, data reduction and lastly argumentation. We began by sorting the data by coding the information that was obtained from the interviews in different themes and tables. According to Bryman and Bell (2011) the coding process is the start point for most forms of qualitative research that is crucial, since it implies managing data that is either categorized, separated, or compiled. We structured the empirical data by categorizing it based on three different themes which were cybersecurity, risk awareness, and roles and responsibilities.

The reason behind this structure is that we wanted the empirical data to follow the same structure as the theoretical framework. Which begins by describing cybersecurity and cyber incidents that are later followed by the description of the top management and its role in cybersecurity and lastly the risk awareness that includes the knowledge and organizational culture. In each theme we identified the main concepts that we compiled in a table with a respective representation of the respondents to see whether some concepts were repeated by other respondents or not. This was made to create an understanding of which common concepts that the respondents value the most and were therefore essential for each theme.

After we have categorized the data, it was time to consider the relevance of the empirics to further exclude the data that was not relevant for the analysis. Alvehus (2013) describes that the data need to be compressed in the sense that information that is less important for the study is briefly described while the one that is being considered important for the analysis is described with a greater level of detail. Therefore, the empirics that did not have any theoretical coverage were considered irrelevant and therefore excluded. Due to the focus of the theoretical conceptualization that is the tone from the top and the risk awareness perspective the empirics that could be related to these concepts in the analysis were kept with an elevated level of detail. When the reduction of the empirics was done, we moved forward with the argumentation which is in other words, the analysis.

For the analysis that is presented in *Chapter 5,* a grounded theory is used containing an approach that is widely used for the analysis of qualitative data (Bryman and Bell, 2011). In the analysis, the theoretical conceptualization that has previously been developed in *Chapter 2* was applied to the empirical data that has been collected through the interviews and tested against it. We have decided to structure the analysis according to the theoretical conceptualization, shown in *Figure 2,* which means that the chapter is divided into four sections. In the first section we analyze the importance of the tone from the top in cybersecurity. In the second section we analyze the influential factors with the relation to the tone from the top. Further in the third section we analyze cybersecurity requirements with relation to the tone from the top where the analysis is focused on knowledge and the organizational culture. Lastly in the fourth section we analyze the consequences of a lacking cybersecurity with relation to the tone from the top, to give an understanding of the possible outcome of not having a sufficient level of cyber risk awareness. This structure has been chosen because it reflects the model for the theoretical conceptualization that is based on the three main themes that this study has. That is the cybersecurity, the top management and the risk awareness that emphasizes the knowledge and organizational culture. Therefore, every section of the analysis corresponds to a certain part of the model.

3.6 Quality Aspects

This book follows a qualitative research method which implies that the researcher has a more involved role in the research process in comparison to the quantitative research. This research method also implies that the quality measures cannot be tested through any external instruments but are solely made by the researcher's judgement (Golfashani, 2003; Patton, 2002). Despite that, the quality aspects need to be demonstrated regardless of the type of research method used (Patton, 2002). We decided to structure this book quality discussion based on Alvehus (2013) that implies a discussion of validity and reliability. Validity according to Brink (1993) investigates the trustworthiness and accuracy which means that the study investigates what it was supposed to investigate. The author further makes a distinction between internal and external validity that we will discuss later in this section. Reliability on the other hand assesses the stability, consistency of the research process in which the repeatability of the results is examined (Alvehus, 2013; Guba and Lincoln, 1994). These two concepts together with objectivity will be further discussed to examine the quality level of this research. Because according to Whittemore et al. (2001) the research must have a true value, be applicable, consistent and natural to be considered valuable.

3.6.1 Credibility: Internal validity

Credibility can also be referred to as internal validity, which according to Golafshani (2003) is the criteria that refers to the degree to which the research can be considered believable and credible from the participants' perspective. To obtain that, the respondents were given space during the interviews to convey their point of view on the matter. We were aware that the respondents came from different professional backgrounds which therefore implied different perspectives and opinions on cyber risk awareness and the top management. Because we both interviewed researchers and on the other hand the cybersecurity consultants, we made sure that both types of participants could express their opinion by providing them with open interview questions. Because it is crucial that the findings therefore reflect reality and not be an outcome caused by an external variable (Brink, 1993). Hence, to reflect the reality it was important for us to have an equal representation of the respondents that are considered experts in the private sector and researchers that take place in public institutions. Because we were aware that the experts could have a neutral perspective on the subject while the experts could have a perspective that was shaped by their occupation.

3.6.2 Transferability: External validity

According to Golafshani, (2003) transferability refers to the degree to which the data obtained in the research can be generalized and transferred to other contexts and settings. This study has been done in a management context that emphasized the business approach by a constant focus. According to Shenton (2004), qualitative studies tend to be rather specific than generalizing, based on the fact that the size of the sample is lower in a qualitative research than in a quantitative one the qualitative studies are usually specific to a small number of the population which therefore makes it difficult to transfer it into a different context. Our study includes eleven participants which enables us to make a realistic generalization of the empirics. Hence, Bryman and Bell (2011) highlights that the type of data that is obtained from both research methods differs in depth. This implies that the results given by studying our questions from a management perspective might not be relatable in other contexts. Therefore, we aim to describe an overall picture of the components the data contributes with, giving the reader the opportunity to apply the research in another context based on his/her perception, a perspective given by Bryman and Bell (2011).

3.6.3 Dependability: Reliability

Dependability implies that the results are consistent and repeatable which means that even with a re-examination of the study the results would be the same (Shenton, 2004). Therefore, dependability according to Golafshani (2003) and Moon et al. (2016) examines the trustworthiness of the research process in which the completed research procedures are examined that allows the reader to follow the particular research process. To achieve a high level of reliability, a high dependability is required (Bryman and Bell, 2011). Therefore, according to the authors, it is important to document the components of the study, including for example the selection of respondents. Moon et al. (2016) state that the researcher should document the research design and its implementation and the data collection process. For that reason, we have intended to be transparent with the procedures that have been applied in the research process by describing them thoroughly in the method section. In which we describe the research design, the data collection process, the analytical method, the quality, and the ethical considerations. Another example is that we both made sure to record the interviews through a recording device and transcribe them afterwards. After each interview, we have decided to exchange recordings in case of eventual technical problems.

3.6.4 Confirmability: Objectivity

Confirmability according to Golafshani, (2003) refers to the extent in which the data that have been collected in research can be confirmed by others. To fulfill the confirmability, we made sure to provide the participants with the same information before the interview. So that everyone had the same starting point. Although we strive to maintain objectivity in the research, Hoepfl (1997) claims that it is impossible to remain objective in qualitative research due to its reliance on interpretations. The author states instead that a researcher should strive for neutrality. A research that is neutral is striving to not be judgmental and present the finding in a balanced way (Hoepfl, 1997). To achieve neutrality in the research we have presented the empiric so that it reflects what has been stated by the respondents during that interview. The only exclusion of the empirical data has been based on its relevance in relation to the theoretical framework. We also strived to base the opinion on the theoretical framework and exclude any personal views and opinions in the presentation of the empiric and further in the analysis.

3.6.5 Criticism of sources

One of the criteria to decide the relevance of sources is freedom of tendency, which according to Thurén (2013) means that the source should not give false information and aim to exclude subjectivity. To take this into consideration, the articles that have been used in this book were carefully selected, placing a presence on them to be peer-reviewed. This according to Bryman and Bell, (2011) means that the articles have been reviewed and approved by specialists in specific research fields. The articles have been obtained through the databases that have been described at the beginning of *Chapter 3*. Besides peer-reviewed articles, we have also used sources run by the government or corresponding institutes operating in cybersecurity. These sources were mainly the Swedish Civil Contingencies Agency (MSB) and Security and Defense Companies (SOFF). Another criteria that we wanted to fulfill is time casualization, where the majority of our sources proceed from later years. However, since cybersecurity is a relatively new topic, a small number of older sources were used to broaden the picture and vary the perspectives.

3.7 Ethical considerations

Research ethics is mainly about finding balance between different types of interest, the knowledge interest is one of them. New knowledge is a valuable resource that can contribute to the development on the individual and societal level. Although some types of research to obtain new knowledge may carry some risk for the participants. Therefore, it is as important to protect the participants from potential risks (Vetenskapsrådet, 2017).

Research ethics concerns questions concerning how the respondents' data is treated and the information given to the respondents (Diener and Crandall, 1978). The ethical considerations that have been considered during the conduction of this study are that cybersecurity for many companies and respondents might be a sensitive topic. Therefore, we have decided to protect the integrity of the respondents by keeping their identities anonymous, in line with Bryman and Bell (2011).

To assure the data and privacy protection of the respondents we have taken into consideration the General Data Protection Regulation (GDPR) which is the data protection regulation of the neutral persons personal data that have been established by the European Union (European Union, 2016). According to Vetenskapsrådet (2002), there are four components of research ethics, namely that the interviewers must provide the respondents information about the aim of the study, the interviewer needs to inform about the conditions they are going to participate in. Therefore, we made sure to inform the respondents how the material obtained during the interviews will be used in our book. All this information was given to each respondent before the interview started, and by receiving their consent, the recording and the interview procedure began. Further, the third component presented by Vetenskapsrådet (2002) states that data of the respondents is to be treated confidentially and finally the data must be treated only in accordance with the study. Since our purpose was to conduct empirical data from the interviews, there was also no reason for us to mention the identities of the respondent nor their companies or projects. We worked in accordance with the Vetenskapsrådet (2017) report when presenting the empirics and the respondents in our book. The report states that the connection between the individual's identity and their statement should be eliminated and should not be able to be re-established by any external parties. We also made sure to get the respondents approval before recording the interviews and gave them the option of not being recorded.

3.8 Method criticism

Having semi-structured interviews as a method is time-consuming, since 45 minutes, for instance, required approximately five hours to transcribe, in accordance with Bryman and Bell (2011). As the authors further state, the quality of the interviews can be enhanced when physically making it possible to read body language etc. This in our case was not possible, although there was still space for nodding, smiling, or expressing other facial impressions through the video interviews. Bryman and Bell (2011) also mention that one might be taking the risk that the respondent ends a phone call if he or she feels uncomfortable during a phone interview. Only one of our interviews was through a phone call, but the respondents still had the option to end a video meeting if wanted. Nevertheless, it might require more effort to do so in comparison with a phone call.

Another perspective of method criticism is that we interviewed experts regarding the cybersecurity of Swedish companies, which means that our data is based on their point of view. If we would have interviewed a company about their own cybersecurity, the answers given to us might have differed giving a relatively more positive approach. Another potential weakness is that since our interview respondents are well-informed on the topic and have had a long work experience related to it, they might have their own ideas and assumptions about how Swedish companies are treating their cybersecurity. This in turn debilitates the objectivity of the empirical data. However, Eisenhardt and Graebne, (2007), mention that to avoid subjectivity and to grasp the whole picture, there is a need to include different kinds of respondents from different companies. Therefore, to decrease the level of subjectivity, our 11 respondents each came from different organizations, chosen on the basis of a wide variety, including science parks, consultancies, and top management in private companies. Another intent to keep the data as objective as possible was made by asking the respondents why they answered in a certain way. This made it possible for us to analyze their intentions with the data.

4. Empirical Findings

4.1 Cybersecurity

4.1.1 The importance of cybersecurity

When asking the respondents about the relevance of cybersecurity in a company, there was an agreement that the reason was the digitalization of society which means that the need for cybersecurity is constantly increasing. Respondents A, F, G and I, meant that cybersecurity is a requirement for a well-functioning digitalization and society. Respondent J meant that digitalization makes the information easily accessible for foreign powers who can take advantage and steal the innovation, patent, and knowledge. This is also something that respondents A, B, and D described. According to them, Sweden is a country that is at the forefront when it comes to innovation and it is, therefore, something that should be protected.

Respondent A even stated that cybersecurity should be of national interest to protect innovation, knowledge, and patents because it contributes to the Swedish economy. Respondents E, G, and J further claimed that cybersecurity is important because it affects every actor in the society, those are the state, the organization, and the consumers. The respondent explained that on the state level it is about stability, on the organizational level it is about the business climate and the prevention of internet crimes and lastly, on the consumer level, it is about democracy and legal safety. Another reason that makes the topic important according to respondent K, is that cybersecurity is a new subject that is unfamiliar to many. This, therefore, makes it more relevant today as an organizational topic.

Respondents C and H had a different approach, they stated that cybersecurity is important because it has a direct impact on the organization when it comes to protecting valuable information that the company possesses and with that prevents bankruptcy.

4.1.2 Insufficient knowledge among companies

The respondents addressed that there is insufficient knowledge among companies regarding cybersecurity. They claimed that there is a need for more practical and empirical knowledge from the organizational and managerial perspective. Respondents A, B, D, I, and K emphasize that focus should be directed toward investigating cultural understanding and human behavior in the process of cybersecurity because these are the parts that are still lacking knowledge. Respondent K further continued that there is also a need to focus more on the organization where the research should look at the administrative side of cybersecurity, which is to lead the process, control it, follow it up, and create policies, etc. Respondents E, F, G, and H on the other hand claim that since cybersecurity is a new subject there is a need for all kinds of knowledge including everything from the basic examination of the subjects to skills supply. It needs to be updated in every aspect.

4.2 Risk awareness

4.2.1 Importance of risk awareness

The respondents were asked about how they perceive the level of risk awareness in Swedish companies. Overall, the opinions were divided, some stated that the risk awareness has increased because of several factors while most respondents argued that although there was an improvement in risk awareness it is not sufficient. Respondents A, C, and D clearly stated that the level of risk awareness depended partly on the industry although even more pointed to the size of the organizations. They meant that larger organizations operating in for example the financial sector, tend to invest more in the IT department. Nevertheless, respondent A and C stated that even smaller companies need to have a moderate level of cybersecurity, since these are many times still connected to a big company in one way or another, by for example being their suppliers. As a result of not protecting their data, the attacker can access important information about the bigger company through the smaller one, due to lower barriers of protection.

Respondent C and B further stated that risk awareness requires continuous work which should therefore be in the company's interest to discuss daily. Respondent E argued that the number of companies that have been exposed to cyber incidents have increased during the last year, but the risk awareness increases with the exposure to cyber incidents. Further, the respondent claimed that the number of articles about cybersecurity has also increased which implies that the interest for it is higher. However, there is a lack of competence in the labor market due to the fact that more people with this type of competence are in demand. At the same time, the interest in cybersecurity education is also increasing. Hence, organizations started to hire CISO or information security managers. In addition to that, more companies hire cybersecurity consultants. Respondent E finishes off by saying that the number of cyber incidents has unfortunately increased which according to respondent F means that it is because the basic security level is low. Although recent statistics have shown that more companies have learned to not click on unknown links. This means that certain types of cyber incidents may at least decrease and that it is something positive according to respondent E.

4.2.2 Reasons behind the lack of risk awareness

When it comes to the reasons that lead to a lacking risk awareness among the organization's respondents B, C, D, H, I, J and K agreed that the lack of knowledge is a crucial factor when it comes to risk awareness. According to respondents D, H, I, and K, the lack of knowledge means that the ability to identify and evaluate risk is very low which further results in the organization not putting enough effort into the prevention of the risks. Respondent D also argues that the main reason for lacking risk awareness in an organization is the human factor. Humans are the weakest link because of the lack of knowledge regarding the cyber consequences one person can make the whole system go down by clicking on a link. Respondents B, C, and J on the other hand stated that a company either has a sufficient level of knowledge or it is lacking it. This further means that when there is an insufficient level of knowledge in the organization the subject is not prioritized enough because the organizations tend to question why a cyberattack would affect them and be convinced that it would not happen to them.

Respondent G agreed that the main reason is the lack of prioritization by the top management. The lack of resources is also something that respondent B and K described. They claimed it to be an important factor because without resources, no investment can be done. Although respondent B makes a difference between organizations that lack abilities because of their size and those whose top management does not prioritize the issue. Therefore, respondents E, I, and K state that the responsibility for a lacking risk awareness lies on the CEO and the top management. They mean that it is their responsibility as the leaders of the organization to put necessary resources and create policies that benefit the risk awareness and cybersecurity in the company.

Although the reason that the CEO and the top management do not take any actions to foster risk awareness according to respondent K is that they do not possess enough knowledge and because usually an investment in risk awareness and cybersecurity does not have the profit that a usual investment does. The top management tends to see it as a cost that is associated with an abstract risk that is difficult to identify, according to respondent K. However respondent F had a different perspective on the top management and explained that the lack of risk awareness depends on wrong decisions that are mainly influenced by the external environment. This brings a need to investigate the information flow and the competencies among the decision-making.

Respondent A even stated that the fundamental reason for a lacking risk awareness among Swedish companies depends on the Swedish culture. People in Sweden find it hard to imagine that someone would want to harm them in any possible way. The respondent further agrees with respondents B, C, and J when it comes to that the organizations tend to think that cyber risk will not affect them because they do not want to accept to think that someone is interested in hurting their business by stealing their information.

4.2.3 Current state of risk awareness

When looking at the current state of risk awareness among Swedish companies, the respondents had different opinions regarding it. There were only a few respondents who gave a clear yes or no response. Among those who gave a clear no were respondents A, D, I, and J who stated that many companies are unaware of the risks because they do not understand why someone would like to access their systems and information. At the same time respondent, A expressed that organizations have insufficient risk analysis that does not show the adequate state of the risks. The risks are perceived as cost-driven, claimed respondent A. This makes the topic unpopular among the top management and instead, they choose to put greater importance on generating profit to the company and to present cost-effective numbers during the year. This in turn causes a lack of long-term thinking which further has its roots in the culture, states respondent A.

Respondent J explained that usually big companies operating in the IT and the financial sector can be quite aware of the risks, but they do not have direct communication to the top management, which makes it difficult to convey important issues. As a result, it hinders the company to carry through any improvements that would support the awareness. The remaining respondents stated that risk awareness depends on factors such as the size of the organization or the industry. Respondents F, G, and H explained that risk awareness has increased during the past years, but the level often depends on the size of the organization. Large organizations tend to be more aware generally speaking with the increase in size. Continuing the respondents mean that small and medium sized organizations usually lack risk perception significantly.

Despite company size, a larger number of respondents stated that the industry is more crucial for the level of risk awareness. Respondents E, F, and G explain that the military industry, finance industry, and the technology industry to some extents are those who have the highest awareness. The reason for that is that they have always been working on their security and they have done it sustainably. The industries that mostly lack any risk awareness are the public sector and especially minor authorities on the regional level, for example, the healthcare sector which usually does not follow any security principles at all. Although the remaining industries are generally very unaware. Those respondents who stated that Swedish companies are generally aware to a certain extent are B, C, and K. Respondent B explained that overall, the awareness among the organizations has increased. Nevertheless, respondent K stated that the organizations have the basic knowledge about cybersecurity, but they lack information about the consequences that the risk can bring to the company.

4.2.4 Assessment of the current state of cybersecurity among companies

The respondents were asked to, based on their experience, provide an assessment of whether the organizations possess the necessary tools and requirements in terms of knowledge to manage a sudden cyber incident. The majority of the respondents had a clear answer to it and it was, no. Respondent G, I, K, J, F, D, and A all agreed that companies lacked the adequate tools to manage a sudden cyber crisis. Respondent G and F pointed out that companies do not want to put their time and effort into it. Respondent I described instead that organizations prefer to seek external help when a cyber incident occurs instead of investing it internally in the company from the start to prevent it. Respondents A and K state instead that whether an organization possesses suitable tools depends on the industry. Organizations in industries like the national defense or technology often have the adequate skill set to manage unpredictable cyber incidents. Respondent K further stated that mature and large organizations are always better prepared than young and small ones.

Respondent J, on the other hand, presented a different approach. The respondent explained that there are three kinds of protection styles in a company. The first one is those who are unaware of the risks and who do not invest in cybersecurity at all. They do not possess any tools, processes, or knowledge regarding possible risks and their consequences. The second type consists of those who are compliance-driven, which signifies those who only invest enough to live up to the regulations' criteria. These companies are neither secure nor prepared because their investment is still not enough. They usually need a slightly higher investment to be fully secure and they would need to work with security daily and not only when they need to fulfill regulation. Their investment stops as soon as they become compliant.

The third kind the respondent described, is those who are fully aware and therefore fully secure with all tools needed to manage any cyber incident that comes up. Respondent J stated, "If you work with safety, you are always compliant, while if you only work with compliance, you are never safe" (Respondent J). Lastly respondent H claimed that the investment in management tools depends on the type of cyber incident that occurred and that if the company does not have the suitable tools, they have to at least have an understanding of the different types of cyber incidents that can occur so that when it happens, they can respond quickly.

4.3 The top management's role

4.3.1 Motives that drive the top management to maintain risk awareness and cybersecurity

When asked to identify the main motives that bring the top management of a company to prioritize working and elaborating reliable cybersecurity, the respondents agreed that it is directly related to the survival of the organization. Respondent E pinpointed it as the primary motive for the top management to implement a plan of managing a cyber incident, especially for companies that do not possess a wide economic buffer. In the meanwhile, the reason why respondent A attended that the company's survival might be threatened by lacking cybersecurity, is that attackers can reveal the unique selling point and thereby steal the patent, without the organization noticing it. This point of view was also shared by respondent F, who emphasized that the patent of a company is their intellectual capital and losing it to external parties does not only affect the company negatively but also the country.

Depending on the innovation, leakage of information can result in external powers taking advantage of the inventions of Swedish companies. A third perspective presented by respondent G is that company survival is highly dependent on relations with stakeholders, and peculiarly clients. The respondent highlighted that losing the client's trust leads the company in one direction, that is, going bankrupt. Nevertheless, respondent G meant that the assessment of the client for the company does not only depend on whether it is exposed for a cyber incident or not but how it handles the situation and manages the incident while and after being attacked.

4.3.2 Actions to minimize the risk of cyber incidents

The respondents were asked to name specific actions that the top management of a company can take to reduce the number of cyberattacks. Respondents A, B, D, G, and J agreed that raising risk awareness among the top management per se is a decisive factor. Another solution, presented by respondent B, G, I, and J is prioritizing the question of cyber incidents and implementing it as a regular part of maintaining a company, taking into consideration the time, effort, and costs required just like any other essential part to keep the company existing. Respondent A highly emphasized the fact that raising awareness among the management is crucial and clearly expressed that if the management does not take these questions seriously, the option of changing the managing director is to be considered. Respondent I mentioned that cybersecurity constitutes a part of the risk management, comparing it to a company's fire risk management. Although, the respondent asserted that the difference between risk management of a potential fire or a potential cyber incident is that the latter belongs to a constantly changing and developing area, which requires the experts forming its security to always update their information basis and elaborate it accordingly.

Furthermore, respondent B, claimed that raising risk awareness about the subject among the top management should rely on a deep analysis of why the company should have cybersecurity and what it is aiming to protect. The respondent continued that companies often prioritized their cybersecurity to reduce their regular costs, by not buying for example a security solution. Further, respondent B expressed that cybersecurity should not be disregarded based on that reason and that companies are instead to identify certain roles and responsibilities both among the management themselves but also through delegating them downwards, to structure up stable cybersecurity. Both respondents A and B considered the economic costs being higher for experiencing a cyber incident that the company is unprepared for, in comparison with economically prioritizing the task from throughout the regular risk management process.

Sharing the opinion that the top management should raise awareness about cybersecurity, respondent D proposes that it should be done through education, directed to both the management and employees. This education should inform about the possible consequences of not maintaining cybersecurity, to make each member of the organization thoroughly understand why it is important. The respondent further suggests collaboration with competitors by forming educational programs for common use, a perspective that is shared by respondent H. This kind of cooperation is fully possible because it is not directed to the clients, but to create a safe digital environment for the operations of the companies, claimed respondent D. While respondent G also agreed on the point about raising awareness among the members of the management, the respondent also asserted that responsibility should be delegated to the right organization members. Asking an employee to manage the company's cybersecurity without that person possessing the knowledge and tools to carry out the task is not going to contribute, according to respondent G. Instead, the respondent shared the same point of view, of raising the education level for all employees in the company, by first practicing the *why* of protecting the digital data of the company and which information is worth protecting, which the respondent calls "proper" risk analysis.

Another option the respondent named is that the company forms an overriding checklist of the basal factor to take into consideration for a sustainable cybersecurity. Additionally, respondent J claimed that except for raising awareness about the topic, the top management ought to prioritize allocating resources such as time and financial ones to have a decent level of cybersecurity. Another approach added by respondent I is for the top management to identify the main external threats against the intellectual capital of the company and thereafter shape security hygiene, as the respondent chooses to call it. "It is all about combining security with applicable security measures", respondent G.

As for respondent E, an emphasis on two factors was made clear. The first one is to have a continuous inspection to discover potential cyberattacks. The respondent meant that the management must possess knowledge about the company's digital network, including how the systems are integrated, and the inflow and outflow of information and the digital tubes used frequently. Knowing this, it becomes easier to discover an atypical activity and thereby investigate and also identify potential hackers. The second element is to build up a stable incident management ability which allows the company to rapidly react to the attack, counteract its deployment and restore the systems.

4.3.3. The top management's responsibility

All respondents agreed that the main responsible for functioning cybersecurity in a company is the Chief Executive Officer. Nevertheless, they were asked to identify additional specific roles in the management and the company, that certain responsibilities are delegated to. Based on the information given by respondent E, there are three levels in an organization that are responsible for its cybersecurity. These are the strategic, the operative, and daily work. It is the top management's responsibility to make the strategic decisions, and therefore its members must get the facts needed to make adequate choices.

Thereafter, the responsibility is followed by the operative level, where a responsible leader is to delegate the tasks to employees who enforce the decisions in daily actions. These employees can for example be IT technicians who inspect and update the digital systems. Respondent E meant that every single level of these is as important as the other and needs to consociate. As opposed to respondent E, respondent C, considers the Chief Technology Officer (CTO), the Chief Information Officer (CIO), and the development organizations as the most responsible. Additionally, respondent F mentioned that the Chief Information Security Officer´s (CISO) role is significant in this area and that he or she together with line managers should cooperate to preserve a security structure that lives up to the adequate criteria.

Furthermore, respondent C adds a different approach by claiming that although it is the top management's role to form the adequate level of cybersecurity, it is often based on the client's requirement and therefore the client also plays an important role in a company's level of cybersecurity. The respondent claimed that it is partly the client's responsibility to demand an appropriate grade of data protection. Respondents D, E and F meant that this point of view is naive, meaning that the client does not and cannot possess all the information needed to demand a certain level of data protection.

Another perspective presented by respondents D and H is that every employee ought to acquire the relevant knowledge and understand the company's cybersecurity. This point of view is motivated by the argument that any member of staff can be a potential target for external parties to access the company's vulnerable information, respondent D stated. However, respondent H holds the top management as main responsible for the company's cybersecurity, but still asserts that all staff members should have a basic understanding of the subject.

Moreover, CEOs possess outrageous responsibility, because they bear the financial resources required and the mandate to control how the resources are allocated. These resources should be assigned to the security response, and the rest of the employees should be educated regarding cybersecurity. Respondent K disagrees with this statement by claiming that it is risky to assign the main responsibility to one single organizational member and that instead, an interaction of different organizational roles, is the right choice. The respondent further highlighted the fact that IT chiefs many times focus on operative questions that are not connected to security and that it depends on the resources devoted to him or her.

Respondent I claim that in big companies, it is the CEO who is mainly responsible for cybersecurity, but he/she delegates the responsibility to the CISO and he/she, in turn, divides it between the IT responsibilities. However, the respondent suggested that if the IT responsibilities detect a cyber incident or any suspected problems, they should report it directly to the CISO and the top management, and not to any economy chiefs along the way. Those tend not to give the task enough prioritization due to their focus on economic costs, which can result in the problem evolving.

4.3.4. Consequences of a lacking cybersecurity

There was an agreement among the respondents, showing that the worst consequence of lacking cybersecurity is the company going bankrupt. Respondent E pinpointed that if the company does not have sufficient cybersecurity, it might not discover smaller cyberattacks and with time there might occur other hidden incidents that cause information leakage. According to the respondent, it can take up to 236 days on average to discover an infringement, leading to a high amount of information being exposed. The respondent adds that a hacker sometimes waits on the appealing situation and assaults on the exact right second.

According to respondent B, deficient cybersecurity leading to significant cyber crises can cause a bankruptcy of a company, due to destroyed confidence from the stakeholders, and especially from the client's side. It is breaking the promise the company made to the client, to protect their private information. This in turn leads to the consumer turning to competitors, which worsens the situation for the company in question even more. The respondent claimed that it's not only the client's confidence the company is losing but also the reliance of their employees. Respondent A asserted that except for the information leakage, the patent of the company can be stolen, and it has to pay a huge amount of indemnity. Furthermore, respondent D expressed the risk of high economic costs and the deterioration of the brand due to the loss of the client's confidence. When it comes to respondent K, it appears that it depends on the sector the company is devoting its activities to and that in some sectors the risk level of cyber incidents is lower. Nevertheless, the respondent expressed that many companies today are exposed to these kinds of risks and should take them into account to not lose their relations with clients and cause a brand deterioration.

4.4 Empirical summary

The following table summarizes the empirical data that have been presented previously in this chapter where it highlights the essential information that has been said during the interviews.

Table 2: Empirical summary

Topics	Results from the interviews
Cybersecurity	
The importance of cybersecurity	Digitalization of society Protection of assets Affects every actor in the society
Current knowledge insufficiency	Higher understanding of human behavior A new topic that requires higher investments
Risk awareness	
Importance of risk awareness	The level of risk awareness depends on the industry and the size of the organization. The risk awareness has overall increased although the increase is not high enough because simultaneously the number of cyber incidents has increased
Reasons behind the lack of risk awareness	Lack of knowledge Lack of risk prioritization Lack of resources Lack of emphasis from the top management level
Current state of risk awareness among organizations	There is an overall lack of risk awareness among organizations. The level of risk awareness depends on the industry. The level of risk awareness depends on the size of the organization
Current state of cybersecurity among companies	Lack of cybersecurity preparation among companies although the level of preparation depends on the size and industry
The top management's role	
Motives that drive the top management to maintain cybersecurity	Survival of the organization Protection of the unique selling point and patents Relations with the stakeholders
Actions to minimize the risk of cyber incidents	Raise awareness on the top management level. Prioritize and invest in cybersecurity. Conduct risk analysis Cooperate with the competitors. Systematic work and update of the security
Responsible for a functioning cybersecurity	CEO Top management, Security chiefs, IT chiefs
Consequences of a lacking cybersecurity	Bankruptcy Loss of clients and other stakeholders Information leakage and a steal of patents Increased economic costs

5. Analysis

This chapter presents the analysis of the empirics in relation to the theoretical conceptualization that is presented in Figure 2 below. To answer the first research question, what *is the state of cyber risk awareness in Swedish companies and what are the influential factors behind risk awareness?* This book will analyze the influential factors behind the risk awareness and the consequences that the state of the risk awareness can cause, to provide an understanding of why it is important to have a functioning cyber risk awareness. To answer the second research question which is, *why should cyber risk awareness be treated as a top management issue?* This paper will analyze the role of the top management and the cybersecurity requirements that the top management possesses the power to implement to increase cyber risk awareness. The structure of the analysis is based on Figure 2.

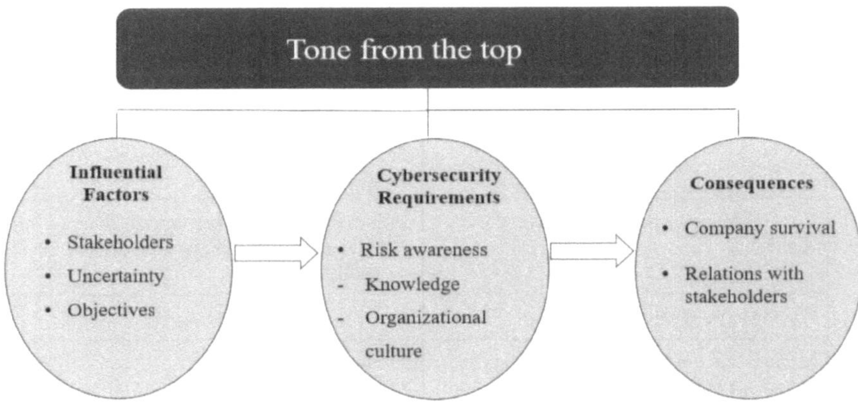

Figure 2. Visualization of the theoretical conceptualization

5.1 The role of the tone from the top

Based on our theoretical conceptualization, the tone from the top, that is the top management starting from the CEO possesses the power to influence the company's culture and thereby the behavior of employees and their attitude towards the company's security. This is based on a top-down approach of risk management (Kelly, 1990; Goel et al., 2020). This statement is reflected in our empirical findings where there is a clear agreement among the respondents that this is the case. However, the empirical findings also suggest that there are several levels except for the strategic one, controlled by the top management. It is indeed the top management who possess the main responsibility, but according to the empirical data, the duties are further delegated to leaders on the operative level, who in turn empower employees to maintain the security on a daily basis, including IT-technicians.

On one hand, some respondents highlighted that all levels are equally important to secure the necessary cybersecurity and that it might be risky to assign the responsibility to only one person. On the other hand, most respondents mentioned roles such as the CEO, CFO, CISO, CTO and CIO as the ones controlling a company's cybersecurity at a structural level. A certain emphasis was still put on the CEO since he/she possesses the financial resources to invest in the company's cybersecurity. The mentioned roles apply to what Beasly et al. (2005), claim where the involvement of the CEO and the CFO have shown to influence the company's enterprise risk management positively, by setting the basis for the organization's risk management. Although our empirical findings are in line with the mentioned authors, they add further detailed roles specific earlier mentioned, in the top management These members also possess a great level of influence on the company's cyber risk awareness, something that the theory leaves behind.

Further empirical findings claim that if the IT-employees on a daily level detect a cyber incident, they are recommended to report the problem directly to the CISO and the top management instead of communicating it to economy chiefs on the operative level. The argument is explained by the claim that these tend to focus on economic costs, which might lead them to ignore the problem. This perspective is also supported by Roberts (1990) where it is argued that middle managers tend to suppress security issues occasionally, resulting in a lower general risk awareness level in the organization. It is thereby most favorable for the company if the issue is directly addressed by the top management. This is also why the top management needs to raise risk awareness among all employees, according to Braumann et al. (2020), which based on the empirical findings can be done through education for both the top management but also all organizational members.

5.2 Tone from the top and the influential factors

Stakeholders

Tone from the top according to Braumann et al. (2020) and Biegelman and Biegelman (2011) is the ultimate factor that affects every part of the risk awareness perspective because the top management has a crucial role when it comes to the initiation and implementation of actions that promote risk awareness. There are certain factors that can influence the top management into taking the appropriate actions. The first influential factor that will be analyzed in this section is the *stakeholders*. As Maharjan and Maharjan (2020) state, the stakeholders have the power to influence an organization. According to the respondents, the assessment of the clients is important because it is directly related to the *company's survival*. The respondents highlighted that when the trust from the stakeholders' side is gone the main outcome from the situation is bankruptcy. This empirical statement is consistent with the claim made by Sinanaj and Zafar (2016), Fombrun and Riel (1997) and Gao et al. (2020) who claim that the stakeholders can both affect the company's reputation when the company does not fulfill its promises, but they can also be affected by it. The reason why the trust is destroyed is because the organization does not deliver what it has promised to the stakeholders. In this sense, the personal and financial information about a client might have been stolen or the patents might have leaked from the company.

As the respondents had highlighted the importance of the stakeholders, the tone from the top should therefore be obligated to take them into account, and as Braumann et al. (2020) and Beasley et al. (2005) claim that the tone from the top cannot function in isolation but there is instead a need for a two-way dialogue. Because of that, the interaction with the stakeholders can lead to mutual learning for both parties. In that way, awareness can be raised from both sides. However, according to the empirical data, the current case does not look like that. Instead, often when there is a lack of awareness in the top management it becomes difficult for the IT department to communicate the issue to the top management, due to a lack of direct communication between these two levels.

The top management therefore possesses the power to and needs to enhance the communication channels between the levels in the organization to be able to raise awareness. According to Kelly (1990), communication has a crucial role when raising risk awareness. To achieve an efficient level of communication it is necessary that the tone from the top according to Biegelman and Biegelman (2011) creates a culture open for a transparent and trustworthy atmosphere that results in an increased open communication between levels. The top management can for instance enable the IT department that has got a higher level of knowledge on the subject, to share it with the rest of the organization.

Objectives

The *objectives* on the other hand according to Naderpour et al. (2014) and Webb et al. (2014) are set by the top management to achieve a certain outcome. According to the empirical data the main motive that influences the top management the most to invest in cyber risk awareness and cybersecurity is the *company's survival*. Although, the theoretical conceptualization that has been developed does not cover it as a one of the influential factors. It is important to be taken into consideration due to the importance that the respondents put on it. The empirical data further states that the survival of the company is threatened by a lack of cybersecurity. This statement is being further analyzed later in this part. Anyhow, the objectives that the organization can set based on the empirical findings can be the protection of the unique selling point, the patents, and the intellectual capital. According to the empirical findings, Sweden is a country with innovative companies, who´s data is worth protecting by sustainable cybersecurity.

Further, the objectives can be different, what is more significant is that they work as a guideline for the whole organization (Naderpour et al., 2014). The protection of the unique selling point could thereby be an objective that works in favor of an increased risk awareness. This can in turn enhance the organization's survival ability because while the unique selling point is protected, the organization's business can be secure. The role of the tone from the top is to make sure that the objectives that are being determined by the organization, are kept relevant for the employees all the time (Braumann et al., 2020; Merchant and Van der Stede, 2017).

As it has been stated by Singh and Kapoor (2016), the main cause of cyber incidents is the human factor and that can also be confirmed by the empirical data. This is hence caused by insufficient level of knowledge among the employees because as the empirical data further states, there is a lack of prioritization of the matter by the top management. As Kelly (1990) states, the process starts with the CEO and what is of importance for him/her is even important to the rest of the organization. Therefore, as many respondents have claimed, the CEO should be held accountable when a company undergoes cyber incidents because it is his/her job to ensure that the organization and its digital assets are being protected. A crucial thing that must be taken into consideration is that either the CEO himself/herself needs to be aware of the possible threats and risks or he/she needs to have sufficient knowledge regarding the issue that makes him/her want to invest in cybersecurity.

Another objective that is favorable for the enhancement of cybersecurity is the nurture of the relations to the stakeholders since they are the key actors for a company's survival (Bauer and van Eeten, 2009). It is therefore important to think about how the company can nurture the relationship. According to the respondents, one way is through enhanced cybersecurity so that the data is protected. As it has been stated earlier, the stakeholders constitute an important role to the company. Therefore, they should also be included in the objectives that the organization determines.

Uncertainty

The influential factor that is left is the uncertainty which according to Istiak and Serletis (2020) imply risk. The lack of ability to predict future risk and threats according to many respondents is the state that many organizations are currently facing. Although Fielder et al. (2018) state that some risks can be predicted through tools like inter alia risk analysis, the empirical findings state that currently, these tools among the organizations are way too insufficient. The digitalization gives an opportunity to technological development according to the Swedish Civil Contingencies Agency (2020). As a result, the methods that are being used in cyber incidents are getting updated. Nonetheless, since there is a lack of interest among the top management regarding cybersecurity, the methods that many organizations use today have not yet been updated in line with the development.

Jen (2012) asserts that the uncertainty can be a motivator for the organizations in raising awareness. Although according to the empirical data many organizations choose to remain in uncertainty when they refuse to believe that someone would want to harm their business. Managers on the top level in companies choose consciously to not believe in the risks and threats and it is a tendency that is claimed to be influenced by the mindset of that nobody would want to harm the company, also asserted to be reflection of the Swedish culture. Besides the cultural aspect that the respondents highlighted, there is once again the lack of awareness that can be explained by the current lack of knowledge. According to Canepa et al. (2021) and Alruwaili (2019), security awareness is a learning process which means that the more an organization knows about cybersecurity, the more aware it becomes about the risks and threats. The respondents claim that it is a new subject and therefore is unknown by many actors.

5.3 Tone from the top and cybersecurity requirements

State of cyber risk awareness

When it comes to the state of risk awareness among Swedish companies, the respondents agreed that it had developed during later years, but that the level is still insufficient and that it is industry and size dependent. Bauer and van Eeten (2009) state that the level of cybersecurity is connected to the stakeholder's requirements that influence a company's incentives to improve it. This even explains the empirical findings implying that the prioritization of cybersecurity is higher in bigger companies and certain industries such as the financial ones. This kind of company possesses a business environment that requires the stakeholders to demand that their data is being protected. One of our respondents even expressed this exact point of view, meaning that it is partly the client's responsibility to demand a certain level of data protection. Nevertheless, this perspective was considered as naive by other respondents, meaning that the client should not and cannot have all the knowledge about how their data is treated by the company, and that it is the company's responsibility to inform the client about that.

Aoyama et al. (2015) states that risk awareness among employees can be raised by security training to minimize human error, but as Prevezianou (2020) means, the managers need to comprehend a crisis to apply the adequate tools to solve it. Among the cybersecurity requirements, Modino et al. (2020) include raising knowledge and risk awareness through hiring experienced people who are conscious of different kinds of threats. This is further supported by the empirical findings expressing that companies tend to involve a CISO in their management to a higher extent nowadays, and they also hire cybersecurity consultants. Still, the overall picture given by the empirical data is that although organizations are taking risk awareness into consideration, the level of investments in it is low outside the financial, technological, and military sector.

However, according to Gao et al. (2020), cyberattacks vary depending on exactly the sector and that thereby the authors state that the measurements to solve the problems should be adjusted accordingly, implying that some sectors have an increased level of requirements to ensure a stable cybersecurity compared to others. Still, the empirical findings elevate the significance of a moderate level of cybersecurity even in for example smaller companies, since those can sometimes be the suppliers for a big company, through which an attacker can access its data. This way, the empirical findings give another approach in comparison with Gao et al. (2020) statement about that organizations are to adjust their cybersecurity according to the industry and their size.

Furthermore, analyzing the empirical data, it does not exactly express that security training is the way to raise risk awareness, although there is an intelligible agreement that the top management should work on raising the educational level in the overall organization about the topic. This will be further discussed under the title *knowledge*.

To achieve the adequate level of cybersecurity and be well-prepared for potential cyber threats, the top management can take some measurements into consideration. The theoretical conceptualization refers to three kinds of aspects including risk awareness, knowledge, and organizational culture, all related to raising risk awareness and thereby cybersecurity. Moreover, the theory indicates that there is a need for an increased level of risk awareness and knowledge about cybersecurity among companies (Goel et al., 2020; Peck et al., 2020; Modino et al., 2020), and the empirical findings precise this requirement by claiming the risk awareness level is to be enhanced not only among employees, but also in the top management per se. The empirical findings even suggest that the management is to consider changing the managing director if he/she does not take implementing sustainable cybersecurity seriously. This past point of view is feasible based on (Prevezianou, 2020) that informs that leaders underestimate cyber threats, which results in them not taking the appropriate management tools, being unaware of the actual risks.

One of the theoretical reasons why situational risk awareness among employees is advantageous for the company is that it leads people to be aware and know what is happening around them resulting in them reacting rapidly in case of detecting any changes (Golandsky, 2016). The empirical data takes this argument a step further by claiming that cybersecurity should be treated in the company's regular risk management, the same way risks for a potential fire are handled. There is a clear linkage between this statement and the information presented in the theory. According to Prevezianou (2020), it is not possible to determine the sense of speed and the ending point of the escalation of a cyber crisis and spread of it to other domains can indeed be rapid. Based on the empirical findings, a logical solution is that the top management includes the cyber risk in the company's regular risk management, preventing it and addressing the adequate measurements in case it happens.

In the end, the empirical data indicate that if the top management raises risk awareness avoids the problem of information leakage that Peck et al. (2020) claim harms a company's reputation. The destruction of the company's reputation can further result in its bankruptcy, based on Sinanaj and Zafar (2016), which based on empirical findings, is avoided by raising risk awareness and the level of knowledge.

Moreover, to develop an appropriate level of risk awareness according to the empirical findings, the top management needs to rely on deep analysis of the underlying factors that cause the company to require cybersecurity and which exact data it is aiming to protect. With a basis in Goel et al. (2020), the top management needs to make strategic and trustworthy decisions to set priorities for which business functions need to be protected. If the top management does not put the effort required, it might be taking enormous risks that could lead to its bankruptcy, which according to the empirical findings is the worst possible consequence of a lacking cybersecurity. Going bankrupt according to the findings is in addition a probable consequence due to the loss of the primary stakeholders, including clients, but also deterioration of brand trust and reputation, loss of patents to unauthorized parties and increased economic costs.

Knowledge is understood to play a crucial role to raise risk awareness regarding cybersecurity. (Jen, 2012 & Sarathchandra et al., 2016). Moreover, Jen (2012) and Mondino et al. (2020) propose awareness as an essential factor to achieve sufficient cybersecurity, and Mondino et al. (2020) suggests that it should be reached through education and thereby an enhanced level of knowledge. The empirical data implies that risk awareness and knowledge go hand in hand, referring to that if the organization defines and knows their general grade of risk tolerance and educates the employees about it, their risk awareness will consequently enhance.

Since the empirical data in addition states that the level of education about cybersecurity is increasing, it implicitly means that there is a positive trend to raise risk awareness among Swedish companies. Nonetheless, the level of knowledge is still not claimed to be sufficient due to most respondent's agreement that lack of knowledge is the main reason for the scar risk awareness, leading to problems in the cybersecurity area. The underlying reason for that according to the empirical findings is the questioning from the company's side of the likelihood of a cyber incident could happen to them. Based on Prevezianou (2020), underestimating cyber threats is the exact problem for why leaders are sometimes hindered from applying the right management tools to protect their data. The knowledge can be increased through risk management training, communication through meetings with focus on risk identification (Jen, 2012; Sarathchandra et al., 2016), facilitating it to create a secure culture (Sarathchandra et al., 2016). A problem some respondents mentioned that is connected to lack of knowledge is the human factor. For example, a person in an organization can cause the whole system to fall just by clicking on an attacker's link, due to a low level of knowledge of what this link can contain, leading to the employees being less aware of the potential problems. In this case, the suggestion of training and having meetings based on (Jen, 2012; Sarathchandra et al., 2016) can be a tool that can be implemented as a cybersecurity requirement to prevent cyber crises.

Moreover, according to the empirical data, Swedish companies need to at least have an overall comprehension of the kinds of cyber incidents that can happen to them, to be able to respond quickly. Being able to respond rapidly also is facilitated by an increased level of knowledge (Gao et al., 2020). Another solution to enhance the organization's information security, according to (Looi, 2005) is that the tone from top can collaborate with competitors, increasing their own knowledge but they can also disclose information about the company's cybersecurity inwardly to their employees. This point of view is shared by the empirical findings where the respondents suggest a collaboration with competitors by forming common educational programs to increase the grade of knowledge. Although Staddon and Easterday (2019) argue that big companies can become vulnerable by disclosing cybersecurity information to their competitors, this kind of collaboration according to the empirical findings is possible and not to be harmful. This is since it is not directed to the clients, but to create a safe digital environment for the operations of the companies.

Organizational culture

The organizational culture is mainly controlled by the top management (Mitrovic et al., 2019), and according to the theory, communicating and discussing cybersecurity issues create a secure environment for the members to attain knowledge on this subject (Sarathchandra et al., 2016). The empirical findings also lift the organization as an important component claiming that cybersecurity affects society including consumers, organizations, and an organizational business climate where the prevention of crimes is actively worked on should be created. Due to cybersecurity being a relatively new topic, many organizations might be unfamiliar with it, which is why they should take it into consideration according to the empirical findings.

Another perspective presented about the organizational culture in Swedish companies, is the statement made by a respondent that includes the general naivety in the Swedish culture that causes companies to reason that no one would be interested in harming their business by stealing their data. Further, the empirical data asserts that it is indeed stealing the company's patent that is one of the aims the attacker has. These statements create an understanding of why organizational culture is such a decisive factor for a company, and to yet clarify its importance based on (Janićijević, 2013), it is the company culture that includes the norms, values, attitudes, and assumptions of the organizational members. Additionally, the author asserts that it helps them comprehend the meaning of their environment. In the case of the study, it is a cyber threat environment, resulting in them identifying the risks they as an organization are exposed for.

5.4 Tone from the top and the consequences of lacking cyber risk awareness

Braumann et al. (2020) states that the top management has a crucial role to influence risk awareness and that it is even something that has been confirmed by the respondents during the interviews. The consequences that the theoretical conceptualization presents can be considered as motives for the top management when raising risk awareness through inter alia increasing the level of cybersecurity within the organization. Gao et al. (2020) presents that a company's survival is one of the consequences of a raised level of risk awareness. According to the empirical data the main motive that the organization has when investing in cybersecurity is company survival, as it has been discussed previously in *Chapter 5.2 Tone from the top and the influential factors.* Not only can an organization have survival as their main motive, but there can also be other objectives that can result in an improved cybersecurity and contribute to the survival of the business. On the other hand, the company's survival is according to Raghavan et al. (2017) dependent on the consumers and its trust toward the organization. This statement is being confirmed by the empirical data which states that the relation to the stakeholders is crucial for the company's survival. Because mistrust from the consumer's side can only lead the company toward bankruptcy. Because as it is stated by Gao et al. (2020) the stakeholders have the power to influence the organization's reputation. The reputation on the other hand according to Sinanaj and Zafar (2016) and Fombrun and Riel (1997) is an asset to the company. The empirical findings confirm that statement by claiming that a destroyed confidence from the stakeholders leads the company only toward bankruptcy.

The empirical data states that many Swedish organizations are unaware about the potential threats and risks that a non-sufficient cybersecurity level may cause. Some are unaware because of the industry that they operate with due to the industry policy Hasan et al. (2021). The empirical findings state that there is still a perception that some industries are more demanded by the external parties than others. Many organizations choose to stay unaware and continuously do not put any resources on cybersecurity or actions that promote risk awareness. Other organizations prefer to seek external help when a cyber incident strikes which corresponds to the claim made by Golandsky (2016). Some respondents state that cybersecurity requires continuous work which is something that many organizations are lacking according to respondent J. The respondent further presented three types of organizations with different levels of cybersecurity. What is important to notice is that the respondent further stated that all many organizations are *fully aware*. Many are just *compliance driven* which still makes them vulnerable to the threats. Further, the empirical data asserts that the number of cyber incidents has increased during the recent year. This fact strengthens the argument that many organizations are still not prepared nor aware of the threats.

Further, the consequences of the negligent behavior that many organizations seem to have can potentially contribute to is the loss of clients and stakeholders, information leakage and theft of patents and lastly an increased economic cost that might lead to a company's bankruptcy. Although the empirical data asserts that the matter of survival is affected by the size of the company. The respondents claim that large organizations, because of the size of their resources, have a chance to survive a potential cyber crisis. Raghavan et al. (2017) states that the stakeholders put a lot of trust in the organization when sharing the personal information about them. A leakage of that information can make them unable to not transact with the organization on terms that are favorable to the business according to Kamiya et al. (2020). Because of that the tone from the top should feel obligated to protect the stakeholders by protecting the information about them. It is important to notice that it is not only the organization that is exposed to risks, but it is simultaneously exposing their stakeholders to it. The empirical data claims that the survival of the organization is highly dependent on the relation to the stakeholders.

6. Conclusion

The purpose of the study is to contribute to an increased understanding of strategic leadership´s influence on cyber risk awareness. The analysis of the questions followed the structural frame of our theoretical conceptualization, explained in *Figure 2*. Starting with the role of the top management, it has been revealed to be crucial, starting with the CEO who possesses the main power to influence the company culture, knowledge and thereby the risk awareness. The top management further delegates the responsibilities to others but is still the main tray of a sustainable cybersecurity puzzle. To raise awareness and knowledge, the top management is suggested to educate both themselves and their employees so that every organizational member is prepared when the circumstances change and can respond rapidly. Another solution is for example collaborating with competitors to enhance the educational knowledge among companies regarding cybersecurity and to raise awareness.

The reason why organizational knowledge is such an important component for a company´s cybersecurity is that it creates the foundation for an open discussion internally, leading to a secure communication ground where knowledge is exchanged and thereby enhanced as a result. However, it is not only the organizational culture that is a crucial component but also the knowledge itself. With a higher level of knowledge about the risks and threats that exist in the cyber world, organizational members avoid committing mistakes such as opening an unknown link which might lead to the whole company´s cyber chain to be exposed. Although the state of risk awareness among Swedish companies is increasing, it is claimed to still be relatively low. It is by knowledge the company reaches enough risk awareness and therefore, the top management in Swedish companies should take risk awareness as a decisive part in their cybersecurity and not underestimate the threats by prioritizing profit over security. If a crisis indeed occurs, the whole business might come to an end. In fact, the company would be taking the risk of deteriorated relationships with stakeholders and bankruptcy.

6.1 Findings

The purpose of the study is to contribute to an increased understanding of strategic leadership's influence on cyber risk awareness. To do so, we aimed to answer two questions, where the first one is *What is the state of cyber risk awareness in Swedish companies and what are the influential factors behind risk awareness?* and the second one is *Why should cyber risk awareness be treated as a top management issue?*

Answering the first question, the current state of cyber risk awareness in Swedish companies is insufficient, although it is increasing. Moreover, the findings further show that cyber risk awareness depends on the size of the company and the industry in which it is active. An insufficient level of cyber risk awareness leads to a deteriorated relations with the stakeholders, leakage of their information, theft of the patents and last but not least bankruptcy. When it comes to the influential factors behind risk awareness, one of the main ones is the stakeholders. The top management needs to maintain their trust, to result in a trustworthy company reputation. Another influential factor is company survival which, the top management, ensures for instance protecting the business core.

To answer the second question, the role of the top management for a functioning cyber risk awareness and thereby cybersecurity is important, since they are the ones implementing the organizational culture, which in turn influences the level of knowledge and cybersecurity. The CEO is held mainly responsible for the cybersecurity of the company, but he/she also delegates to the operative level. Other important roles in the top management when it comes to possessing the adequate knowledge and enhancing cybersecurity are the CFO, CISO, CTO and CIO. Secondly, the top management possesses the actual power to take the actions required for a functioning cybersecurity by improving risk awareness, knowledge and creating an organizational culture where the issue is discussed. They can for example make it possible to involve cybersecurity in the company's regular risk management and to deeply analyze which data the company needs to protect. To enhance knowledge and thereby awareness, the top management has the power to identify the company's risk tolerance about security to and educate employees thereafter by for example security training, and discussions through meetings. Another action that can be taken is to cooperate with competitors to form educational programs about cybersecurity. Finally, the top management can ensure working proactively by setting norms and assumptions about cybersecurity. All these identified reasons explain why the cyber risk awareness should be treated as a top management issue and support it.

As discussed throughout the book, there is a lack of prioritization of risk awareness and cybersecurity from the top management's side, something that might be reflected in the state of risk awareness among Swedish companies. Therefore, treating cyber risk awareness as a top management issue giving it higher prioritization could possibly influence the state of risk awareness positively.

6.2 Contributions

The purpose of the study is to contribute to an increased understanding of strategic leadership's influence on cyber risk awareness. As a contribution to the academic field of management of cybersecurity, this book provides a better understanding of the top management's role in the cybersecurity issues, where it also outlines the management roles that are mainly responsible for the cybersecurity in an organization. It further shows that the top management has the power to influence cyber risk awareness by implementing specific actions but also by creating an organizational culture that increases knowledge about cybersecurity and the possible cyber threats and risks which at the end increases the cyber risk awareness.

Moreover, this paper contributes with a different perspective on cybersecurity by focusing on the management. Cybersecurity is usually treated in the field of IT which does not take the top management into consideration. The data from our respondents who are well informed on this topic, addressed cybersecurity and cyber risk awareness as two connected factors. The overall picture mediated by them is that the top management has great power on a company's cybersecurity, which shifts the attention from discussing the topic only based on advanced digital solutions, and opens up for looking at the human factor, in this case the top management as a decisive component. This study therefore shows the importance of the top management and the power of the right leadership necessary to attain a sufficient cybersecurity level in an organization. It contributes with an insight that it is as important that the top management is aware of cybersecurity as it is to possess the right technical tools to manage it. As we believe it is both the mindset and technical knowledge of the company that influences the protection of data, we hope to see this topic discussed not only from a technical approach, but also with a managerial emphasis.

6.3 Future research

This study focused on researching risk awareness, knowledge, and organizational culture regarding cybersecurity in companies taking into consideration the role of the top management in it. The scope of this book was limited to Swedish companies to make the research feasible within a limited time frame. Therefore, future studies could focus on investigating risk awareness and the impact of the top management on multinational companies, considering the cultural aspect of the country where the company is active. Further, it has been discovered during the research that the matter of cybersecurity is mostly studied from the IT perspective, indicating a lack of business perspective on it. Because of that, future studies could put a greater focus on investigating the subject from a point of view where management, investments and costs are considered. The aim can be to calculate the opportunity cost of not implementing a stable cybersecurity, when a crisis strikes.

7. References

Abraham, C., Chatterjee, D., & Sims, R. R. (2019). Muddling through cybersecurity: Insights from the U.S. healthcare industry. *Business Horizons*, *62*(4), 539–548. https://doi.org/10.1016/j.bushor.2019.03.010

Acar, O. A., Tarakci, M., & van Knippenberg, D. (2019). Creativity and Innovation Under Constraints: A Cross-Disciplinary Integrative Review. *Journal of Management*, 45(1), 96–121. https://doi.org/10.1177/0149206318805832

Alruwaili, A. (2019). A review of the impact of training on cybersecurity awareness. *International Journal of Advanced Research in Computer Science*, *10*(5), 1–3. https://doi.org/10.26483/ijarcs.v10i5.6476

Alvehus, J. (2013). Skriva uppsats med kvalitativ metod. Liber AB, Stockholm. Första upplagan

Aoyama, T., Naruoka, H., Koshijima, I., & Watanabe, K. (2015). How Management Goes Wrong? – The Human Factor Lessons Learned from a Cyber Incident Handling Exercise. *Procedia Manufacturing*, *3*, 1082–1087. https://doi.org/10.1016/j.promfg.2015.07.178

Babbie, Earl (2014). The Basics of Social Research (6th ed.). Belmont, California: Wadsworth Cengage. pp. 303–04.

Backman, S. (2020). Conceptualizing cyber crises. *Journal of Contingencies and Crisis Management.* https://doi.org/10.1111/1468-5973.1234

Bada, M., Sasse, A. M., & Nurse, J. R. C. (2019, January 9). Cyber Security Awareness Campaigns: Why do they fail to change behaviour? *ArXiv. arXiv*

Bakos, L., Dumitraşcu, D. D., & Harangus, K. (2019). Human factor preparedness for decentralized crisis management and communication in cyber-physical systems. *Sustainability (Switzerland)*, 11(23). https://doi.org/10.3390/su11236676

Bauer, J. M., & van Eeten, M. J. G. (2009). Cybersecurity: Stakeholder incentives, externalities, and policy options. *Telecommunications Policy*, 33(10–11), 706–719. https://doi.org/10.1016/j.telpol.2009.09.001

Beasley, M. S., Clune, R., & Hermanson, D. R. (2005). Enterprise risk management: An empirical analysis of factors associated with the extent of implementation. *Journal of Accounting and Public Policy*, 24(6), 521–531. https://doi.org/10.1016/j.jaccpubpol.2005.10.001

Biegelman, M. T., & Biegelman, D. R. (2011). Tone at the Top and Throughout. In *Building a World-Class Compliance Program* (pp. 25–44). John Wiley & Sons, Inc. https://doi.org/10.1002/9781118268193.ch2

Boeke, S. (2018). National cyber crisis management: Different European approaches. *Governance*, 31(3), 449–464. https://doi.org/10.1111/gove.12309

Bontempo, R. N., Bottom, W. P., & Weber, E. U. (1997). Cross-cultural differences in risk perception: A model-based approach. *Risk Analysis*, 17(4), 479–488. https://doi.org/10.1111/j.1539-6924.1997.tb00888.x

Braumann, E. C., Grabner, I., & Posch, A. (2020). Tone from the top in risk management: A complementarity perspective on how control systems influence risk awareness. *Accounting, Organizations and Society*, 84. https://doi.org/10.1016/j.aos.2020.101128

Braumann, E., Grabner, I., & Posch, A. (2018). Walking the Talk in Risk Management: A Complementarity Perspective on How Tone from the Top Influences Risk Awareness. *SSRN Electronic Journal.* https://doi.org/10.2139/ssrn.3230828

Brink, H. I. (1993). Validity and reliability in qualitative research. *Curationis*, 16(2), 35–38. https://doi.org/10.4102/curationis.v16i2.1396

Britten, N. (1999). Qualitative Interviews in Healthcare. In: Pope, C. and Mays, N., Eds., Qualitative Research in Health Care, 2nd Edition, BMJ Books, London, 11-19.

Bryman, A., & Bell, E. (2011). Business research methods. (Third edition) Oxford university press.

Cambridge Dictionary. (28 April 2021). Awareness.
https://dictionary.cambridge.org/dictionary/english/awareness

Cambridge Dictionary. (28 April 2021). Risk.
https://dictionary.cambridge.org/dictionary/english/risk

Cambridge Dictionary (5 May 2021). Top management.

https://dictionary.cambridge.org/dictionary/english/top-management

Canepa, M., Ballini, F., Dalaklis, D., & Vakili, S. (2021). Assessing the effectiveness of cybersecurity training and raising awareness within the maritime domain. In *Inted2021 Proceedings* (Vol. 1, pp. 3489–3499). IATED.
https://doi.org/10.21125/inted.2021.0726

Chatterjee, D. (2019). Should executives go to jail over cybersecurity breaches? *Journal of Organizational Computing and Electronic Commerce, 29*(1), 1–3.
https://doi.org/10.1080/10919392.2019.1568713

Chen, H. S., & Jai, T. M. (Catherine). (2019). Cyber alarm: Determining the impacts of hotel's data breach messages. *International Journal of Hospitality Management, 82*, 326–334. https://doi.org/10.1016/j.ijhm.2018.10.002

Choo, K. K. R. (2011). The cyber threat landscape: Challenges and future research directions. *Computers & security, 30*(8), 719-731.
https://doi.org/10.1016/j.cose.2011.08.004

Colleoni, E., & Arvidsson, A. (2011). Measuring corporate reputation using sentiment analysis. *The 15th International Conference on Corporate Reputation: Navigating the Reputation Economy*, 1–25. Retrieved from
http://openarchive.cbs.dk/handle/10398/8730

Collier, P., Berry, A. J., & Burke, G. T. (2006). Risk and management accounting: best practice guidelines for enterprise-wide internal control procedures. *Risk and Management Accounting, 2*(11), 1–8.

Coombs, W. T., & Holladay, S. J. (2010). *The Handbook of Crisis Communication. The Handbook of Crisis Communication.* Wiley-Blackwell. https://doi.org/10.1002/9781444314885

Dang-Pham, D., Pittayachawan, S., & Bruno, V. (2015). Investigating the formation of information security climate perceptions with social network analysis: A research proposal. In *Pacific Asia Conference on Information Systems, PACIS 2015 - Proceedings.* Pacific Asia Conference on Information Systems.

Daud, M., Rasiah, R., George, M., Asirvatham, D., & Thangiah, G. (2018). Bridging the gap between organisational practices and cyber security compliance: Can cooperation promote compliance in organisations? *International Journal of Business and Society, 19*(1), 161–180.

Denscombe, M. (2014). The Good research guide. Maidenhead, England: *McGraw-Hill/Open University Press.*

Diener, E. and Crandall, R. (1978). Ethics in Social and Behavioral Research. Chicago: The University of Chicago Press

Eisenhardt, K. and Graebner, M. (2007). Theory Building From Cases: Opportunities And Challenges. Academy of Management Journal, 50(1), pp.25-32.

Elo, S., & Kyngäs, H. (2008). The qualitative content analysis process. *Journal of Advanced Nursing, 62*(1), 107–115. https://doi.org/10.1111/j.1365-2648.2007.04569.x

Eswaran, R., & Vinayagamoorthi, G. (2019). Cyber security and information security. *International Journal of Recent Technology and Engineering,* 8(3 Special Issue), 372–374. https://doi.org/10.35940/ijrte.C1079.1083S19

European Union. (2016). Regulation 2016/679 of the European parliament and the Council of the European Union. *Official Journal of the European Communities,* 1–88

Fielder, A., König, S., Panaousis, E., Schauer, S., & Rass, S. (2018). Risk assessment uncertainties in cybersecurity investments. *Games,* 9(2). https://doi.org/10.3390/g9020034

Fombrun, C., & van Riel, C. (1997). The Reputational Landscape. *Corporate Reputation Review, 1*(2), 5–13. https://doi.org/10.1057/palgrave.crr.1540024

Forno, R. F. (2019). Risk awareness and the user experience. In *SIGDOC 2019 - Proceedings of the 37th ACM International Conference on the Design of Communication. Association for Computing Machinery, Inc.* https://doi.org/10.1145/3328020.3353918

Freeman, R. E. E., & McVea, J. (2005). A Stakeholder Approach to Strategic Management. *SSRN Electronic Journal.* https://doi.org/10.2139/ssrn.263511

Gao, L., Calderon, T. G., & Tang, F. (2020). Public companies' cybersecurity risk disclosures. *International Journal of Accounting Information Systems, 38.* https://doi.org/10.1016/j.accinf.2020.100468

Goel, R., Kumar, A., & Haddow, J. (2020). PRISM: a strategic decision framework for cybersecurity risk assessment. *Information and Computer Security, 28*(4), 591–625. https://doi.org/10.1108/ICS-11-2018-0131

Golandsky, Y. (2016). Cyber crisis management, survival or extinction. In *2016 International Conference on Cyber Situational Awareness, Data Analytics and Assessment, CyberSA 2016.* Institute of Electrical and Electronics Engineers Inc. https://doi.org/10.1109/CyberSA.2016.7503291

Golfashani, N. (2003). Understanding Reliability and Validity in Qualitative Research. *The Qualitative Report, 8*(4), 597–607. Retrieved from http://nsuworks.nova.edu/tqr http://nsuworks.nova.edu/tqr/vol8/iss4/6 https://nsuworks.nova.edu/tqr/vol8/iss4/6

Government offices of Sweden- Ministry of Justice. (22 June 2017). *A national cyber security strategy.* https://www.government.se/4ada5d/contentassets/d87287e088834d9e8c08f28d0b9dda5b/a-national-cyber-security-strategy-skr.-201617213

Guba, E. G., & Lincoln, Y. S. (1994). Competing paradigms in qualitative research. In N. K. Denzin & Y. S. Lincoln (Eds.), *Handbook of qualitative research* (Vol. 2, pp.

105–117). Sage. Retrieved from http://create.alt.ed.nyu.edu/courses/3311/reading/10-guba_lincoln_94.pdf

Harclerode, M. A., Lal, P., Vedwan, N., Wolde, B., & Miller, M. E. (2016). Evaluation of the role of risk perception in stakeholder engagement to prevent lead exposure in an urban setting. *Journal of Environmental Management*, 184, 132–142. https://doi.org/10.1016/j.jenvman.2016.07.045

Hasan, S., Ali, M., Kurnia, S., & Thurasamy, R. (2021). Evaluating the cyber security readiness of organizations and its influence on performance. *Journal of Information Security and Applications*, *58*. https://doi.org/10.1016/j.jisa.2020.102726

Hathaway, M. (2012). Leadership and Responsibility for Cybersecurity. *Georgetown Journal of International Affairs*, (Special Issue on International Engagement on Cyber: 2012), 71–80.

Hoepfl, M. C. (1997). Choosing Qualitative Research: A Primer for Technology Education Researchers. *Journal of Technology Education*, *9*(1). https://doi.org/10.21061/jte.v9i1.a.4

Hoffmann, P., Schiele, H., & Krabbendam, K. (2013). Uncertainty, supply risk management and their impact on performance. *Journal of Purchasing and Supply Management*, *19*(3), 199–211. https://doi.org/10.1016/j.pursup.2013.06.002

Ikeda, K., Marshall, A., & Zaharchuk, D. (2019). Agility, skills and cybersecurity: Critical drivers of competitiveness in times of economic uncertainty. *Strategy and Leadership*, *47*(3), 40–48. https://doi.org/10.1108/SL-02-2019-0032

Istiak, K., & Serletis, A. (2020). Risk, uncertainty, and leverage. *Economic Modelling*, 91, 257–273. https://doi.org/10.1016/j.econmod.2020.06.010

Jang-Jaccard, J., & Nepal, S. (2014). A survey of emerging threats in cybersecurity. In *Journal of Computer and System Sciences* (Vol. 80, pp. 973–993). Academic Press Inc. https://doi.org/10.1016/j.jcss.2014.02.005

Janićijević, N. (2013). The mutual impact of organizational culture and structure. *Economic Annals*, *58*(198), 35–60. https://doi.org/10.2298/EKA1398035J

Jen, R. (2012). How to increase risk awareness. Paper presented at PMI® Global Congress 2012—North America, Vancouver, British Columbia, Canada. Newtown Square, PA: *Project Management Institute*.

Kamiya, S., Kang, J. K., Kim, J., Milidonis, A., & Stulz, R. M. (2021). Risk management, firm reputation, and the impact of successful cyberattacks on target firms. *Journal of Financial Economics*, *139*(3), 719–749. https://doi.org/10.1016/j.jfineco.2019.05.019

Kankanhalli, A., Teo, H. H., Tan, B. C. Y., & Wei, K. K. (2003). An integrative study of information systems security effectiveness. *International Journal of Information Management*, *23*(2), 139–154. https://doi.org/10.1016/S0268-4012(02)00105-6

Kelly, D. J. (1990). Ethics: The Tone At The Top. *Management Accounting*, 71(10), 12.

Kemper, G. (2019). Improving employees' cyber security awareness. *Computer Fraud and Security*, *2019*(8), 11–14. https://doi.org/10.1016/S1361-3723(19)30085-5

Kovacevic, A., Putnik, N., & Toskovic, O. (2020). Factors Related to Cyber Security Behavior. *IEEE Access*, 8, 125140–125148. https://doi.org/10.1109/ACCESS.2020.3007867

Kraemer, S., Carayon, P., & Clem, J. (2009). Human and organizational factors in computer and information security: Pathways to vulnerabilities. *Computers and Security*, *28*(7), 509–520. https://doi.org/10.1016/j.cose.2009.04.006

Kulikova, O., Heil, R., Van Den Berg, J., & Pieters, W. (2012). Cyber crisis management: A decision-support framework for disclosing security incident information. In *Proceedings of the 2012 ASE International Conference on Cyber Security, CyberSecurity 2012* (pp. 103–112). IEEE Computer Society. https://doi.org/10.1109/CyberSecurity.2012.20

Kwon, J., Ulmer, J. R., & Wang, T. (2013). The association between top management involvement and compensation and information security breaches. *Journal of Information Systems*, *27*(1), 219–236. https://doi.org/10.2308/isys-50339

Lacey, D. (2010). Understanding and transforming organizational security culture. *Information Management & Computer Security*, 18(1), 4–13. https://doi.org/10.1108/09685221011035223

Lee, I. (2021). Cybersecurity: Risk management framework and investment cost analysis. *Business Horizons*. https://doi.org/10.1016/j.bushor.2021.02.022

Lee, S. O., & Seo, H. J. (2019). Conceptualizing the cyber incident event statistics reporting standards. In *International Conference on Advanced Communication Technology*, ICACT (Vol. 2019-February, pp. 672–675). Institute of Electrical and Electronics Engineers Inc. https://doi.org/10.23919/ICACT.2019.8702015

Looi, H. C. (2005). E-Commerce Adoption in Brunei Darussalam: A Quantitative Analysis of Factors Influencing Its Adoption. *Communications of the Association for Information Systems. 15.* https://doi.org/10.17705/1cais.01503

Maharjan, S. K., & Maharjan, K. L. (2020). Exploring perceptions and influences of local stakeholders on climate change adaptation in Central and Western Tarai, Nepal. *Climate and Development*, 12(6), 575–589. https://doi.org/10.1080/17565529.2019.1664377

Marton, F., & Booth, S. (2013). *Learning and Awareness. Learning and Awareness* (pp. 1–224). Taylor and Francis. https://doi.org/10.4324/9780203053690

Merchant, K. A., & Van der Stede, Wim A. (2017). *Management control systems: Performance measurement, evaluation, and incentives.* (Fourth edition). Englewood Cliffs, NJ: Prentice Hall.

Mikes, A. (2009). Risk management and calculative cultures. *Management Accounting Research*, 20(1), 18–40. https://doi.org/10.1016/j.mar.2008.10.005

Mikušová, M., & Horváthová, P. (2019). Prepared for a crisis? Basic elements of crisis management in an organisation. *Economic Research-Ekonomska Istrazivanja* , 32(1), 1844–1868. https://doi.org/10.1080/1331677X.2019.1640625

Mitrovic, D. M., Simovic, O., & Raicevic, M. (2019). The relationship between leadership styles and organizational culture in sport organizations. *Sport Mont*, 17(3), 85–89. https://doi.org/10.26773/smj.191002

Mondino, E., Scolobig, A., Borga, M., & Di Baldassarre, G. (2020). The role of experience and different sources of knowledge in shaping flood risk awareness. *Water (Switzerland)*, 12(8). https://doi.org/10.3390/W12082130

Moon, K., Brewer, T. D., Januchowski-Hartley, S. R., Adams, V. M., & Blackman, D. A. (2016). A guideline to improve qualitative social science publishing in ecology and conservation journals. *Ecology and Society*, *21*(3). https://doi.org/10.5751/ES-08663-210317

Mundy, J. (2010). Creating dynamic tensions through a balanced use of management control systems. *Accounting, Organizations and Society*, *35*(5), 499–523. https://doi.org/10.1016/j.aos.2009.10.005

Naderpour, M., Lu, J., & Zhang, G. (2014). A situation risk awareness approach for process systems safety. *Safety Science*, 64, 173–189. https://doi.org/10.1016/j.ssci.2013.12.005

Panou, A., Ntantogian, C., & Xenakis, C. (2017). RiSKi: A framework for modeling cyber threats to estimate risk for data breach insurance. In *ACM International Conference Proceeding Series* (Vol. Part F132523). Association for Computing Machinery. https://doi.org/10.1145/3139367.3139426

Patton, M. Q. (2002). Qualitative evaluation and research methods (3rd ed.). Thousand Oaks, CA: Sage Publications, Inc.

Peck, S. M., Khan, M. M. H., Fahim, M. A. A., Coman, E. N., Jensen, T., & Albayram, Y. (2020). Who Would Bob Blame? Factors in Blame Attribution in Cyberattacks among the Non-Adopting Population in the Context of 2FA. In *Proceedings - 2020 IEEE 44th Annual Computers, Software, and Applications Conference, COMPSAC 2020* (pp. 778–789). Institute of Electrical and Electronics Engineers Inc. https://doi.org/10.1109/COMPSAC48688.2020.0-166

Pindek, S., Howard, D. J., Krajcevska, A., & Spector, P. E. (2019). Organizational constraints and performance: an indirect effects model. *Journal of Managerial Psychology*, 34(2), 79–95. https://doi.org/10.1108/JMP-03-2018-0122

Prevezianou, M. F. (2021). Beyond Ones and Zeros: Conceptualizing Cyber Crises. *Risk, Hazards and Crisis in Public Policy*, *12*(1), 51–72. https://doi.org/10.1002/rhc3.12204

Radziwill, N., & Benton, M. (2017, July 9). Cybersecurity cost of quality: Managing the costs of cybersecurity risk management. ArXiv. arXiv.

Raghavan, K., Desai, M. S., & Rajkumar, P. V. (2017). Managing Cybersecurity and e-Commerce Risks in Small Businesses. *Journal of Management Science and Business Intelligence*, 9–15. Retrieved from http://www.ibii-us.org/Journals/JMSBI/

Reeves, A., Parsons, K., & Calic, D. (2020). Whose risk is it anyway: How do risk perception and organisational commitment affect employee information security awareness? In *Lecture Notes in Computer Science (including subseries Lecture Notes in Artificial Intelligence and Lecture Notes in Bioinformatics)* (Vol. 12210 LNCS, pp. 232–249). Springer. https://doi.org/10.1007/978-3-030-50309-3_16

Roberts, J. (1990). Strategy and accounting in a U.K. conglomerate. *Accounting, Organizations and Society*, *15*(1–2), 107–126. https://doi.org/10.1016/0361-3682(90)90017-O

Romanosky, S. (2016). Examining the costs and causes of cyber incidents. *Journal of Cybersecurity*, 2(2), 121–135. https://doi.org/10.1093/cybsec/tyw001

Rometty, V. M. (14 May 2015). *New Ways of Thinking about Enterprise Security*. IBM security summit. https://www.ibm.com/ibm/ginni/05_14_2015.html.

Rothrock, R. A., Kaplan, J., & Van Der Oord, F. (2018). The board's role in managing cybersecurity risks. *MIT Sloan Management Review*, 59(2), 12–15

Ruighaver, A. B., Maynard, S. B., & Chang, S. (2007). Organisational security culture: Extending the end-user perspective. *Computers and Security*, *26*(1), 56–62. https://doi.org/10.1016/j.cose.2006.10.008

Sarathchandra, D., Haltinner, K., & Lichtenberg, N. (2016). College Students' Cybersecurity Risk Perceptions, Awareness, and Practices. In *Proceedings - 2016 Cybersecurity Symposium, CYBERSEC 2016* (pp. 68–73). Institute of Electrical and Electronics Engineers Inc. https://doi.org/10.1109/CYBERSEC.2016.018

Schwartz, M. S., Dunfee, T. W., & Kline, M. J. (2005). Tone at the top: An ethics code for directors? In *Journal of Business Ethics* (Vol. 58, pp. 79–100). https://doi.org/10.1007/s10551-005-1390-y

Security and defense companies. (2021). *State sponsored cyber attacks*. Säkerhets- och försvarsföretagen. https://soff.se/wp-content/uploads/2018/03/Cybersecurity_statsunderst%C3%B6dda-akt%C3%B6rer.pdf

Security and defense companies. (February 2021). *Årliga rapporter*. Säkerhets- och försvarsföretagen. https://soff.se/wp-content/uploads/2021/03/lanksamlig_pdf_1.2.pdf

Shenton, A. K. (2004). Strategies for ensuring trustworthiness in qualitative research projects. Education for information, 22(2), ss. 63–75.

Sinanaj, G., & Zafar, H. (2016). Who wins in a data breach? - A comparative study on the intangible costs of data breach incidents. In *Pacific Asia Conference on Information Systems, PACIS 2016 - Proceedings*. Pacific Asia Conference on Information Systems

Singh, A., & Kapoor, B. (2016). Analysis of the Human Factor behind Cyber Attacks. *International Research Journal of Engineering and Technology*, 11, 2395–56. Retrieved from https://www.irjet.net/archives/V3/i11/IRJET-V3I11209.pdf

Sonenshein, S. (2014). How organizations foster the creative use of resources. *Academy of Management Journal*, *57*(3), 814–848. https://doi.org/10.5465/amj.2012.0048

Staddon, J., & Easterday, N. (2019). "It's a generally exhausting field" A Large-Scale Study of Security Incident Management Workflows and Pain Points. In *2019 17th International Conference on Privacy, Security and Trust, PST 2019 - Proceedings*. Institute of Electrical and Electronics Engineers Inc. https://doi.org/10.1109/PST47121.2019.8949012

Summerill, C., Pollard, S. J. T., & Smith, J. A. (2010). The role of organizational culture and leadership in water safety plan implementation for improved risk management. *Science of the Total Environment, 408*(20), 4319–4327. https://doi.org/10.1016/j.scitotenv.2010.06.043

Sung, J., & Hanna, S. (1996). Factors related to risk tolerance. *Journal of Financial Counseling and Planning,* 7, 11–19. https://doi.org/10.2139/ssrn.2234

Swedish Civil Contingencies Agency. (2021). *Cyberhot.* Myndigheten för samhällsskydd och beredskap. https://www.msb.se/sv/amnesomraden/informationssakerhet-cybersakerhet-och-sakra-kommunikationer/cyberhot/

Swedish Civil Contingencies Agency. (2020). *Cybersäkerhet i Sverige – Hot, metoder, brister och beroenden.* Myndigheten för samhällsskydd och beredskap. https://www.msb.se/contentassets/fe72c449466e4017bd76787762ab9dc5/rapport-cybersakerhet-i-sverige-2020--hot-metoder-brister-och-beroenden.pdf

Swedish Civil Contingencies Agency. (2021). *Informationssäkerhetsmånaden.* Myndigheten för samhällsskydd och beredskap. https://www.msb.se/sv/amnesomraden/informationssakerhet-cybersakerhet-och-sakra-kommunikationer/informationssakerhetsmanaden/

Swedish Civil Contingencies Agency. (2020). *Årsrapport, Statliga myndigheters it-incidentrapportering 2020-Utmaningar för en säker och robust informationshantering.* Myndigheten för samhällsskydd och beredskap https://rib.msb.se/filer/pdf/29488.pdf

TRUESEC. (May 2020). *Swedish Cyber Threat Landscape- Cyber threat intelligence report.* https://www.truesec.com/wp-content/uploads/2020/06/Truesec-Swedish-Cyber-Threat-Landscape.pdf

Thurén, T. (2013). Källkritik. 3. uppl., Stockholm: Liber AB

Vardarlıer, P. (2016). Strategic Approach to Human Resources Management During Crisis. *Procedia - Social and Behavioral Sciences, 235,* 463–472. https://doi.org/10.1016/j.sbspro.2016.11.057

Vetenskapsrådet (2002). Forskningsetiska principer inom humanistisk-samhällsvetenskaplig forskning.

Vetenskapsrådet. (2016). God forskningssed. *AIP Advances* (Vol. 6, p. 056119). Retrieved from http://aip.scitation.org/doi/10.1063/1.4944399

Von Solms, R., & Van Niekerk, J. (2013). From information security to cyber security. *Computers and Security*, 38, 97–102. https://doi.org/10.1016/j.cose.2013.04.004

Walker, D. H. T., Bourne, L. M., & Shelley, A. (2008). Influence, stakeholder mapping and visualization. *Construction Management and Economics*, 26(6), 645–658. https://doi.org/10.1080/01446190701882390

Wang, D., Su, Z., & Yang, D. (2011). Organizational culture and knowledge creation capability. *Journal of Knowledge Management*, *15*(3), 363–373. https://doi.org/10.1108/13673271111137385

Webb, J., Ahmad, A., Maynard, S. B., & Shanks, G. (2014). A situation awareness model for information security risk management. *Computers and Security*, 44, 1–15. https://doi.org/10.1016/j.cose.2014.04.005

Whittemore, R., Chase, S. K., & Mandle, C. L. (2001). Validity in qualitative research. *Qualitative Health Research*, *11*(4), 522–537. https://doi.org/10.1177/104973201129119299

Zeier Roeschmann, A. (2014). Risk Culture: What It Is and How It Affects an Insurer's Risk Management. *Risk Management and Insurance Review*, 17(2), 277–296.

Zwilling, M., Klien, G., Lesjak, D., Wiechetek, Ł., Cetin, F., & Basim, H. N. (2020). Cyber Security Awareness, Knowledge and Behavior: A Comparative Study. *Journal of Computer Information Systems*. https://doi.org/10.1080/08874417.2020.1712269